DIAGNOSIS: CANCER!

How My Faith Journey Made Me Whole

Alicia Griffin

Scripture quotations taken from the HOLY BIBLE, NEW
INTERNATIONAL VERSION (NIV) Copyright © 1973, 1978,
1984 by International Bible Society, used by permission; THE
AMPLIFIED BIBLE and AUTHORIZED KING JAMES
VERSION (AV) unless otherwise quoted.

Compiled & Edited by: Lily Mudasia
Cover Design by: D District Media
First Paperback Edition published in 2013
Library of Congress Catalog Number 2013946173
Printed in USA

ISBN NUMBER:978-0-9893295-1-4 Soft Copy
            978-0-9893295-2-1 Hard Copy

Dedication

Dedicated to
The Memory of
My Godmother
Evangelist Adrienne Hayes "Mama A"
(3/23/55-10/29/2012)
You were the pillar that held my heart.

Diagnosis: Cancer

Praise For Diagnosis: Cancer!

One woman, one Word and a wealth of prophecy with unlimited results! Alicia Griffin's book, *Diagnosis, Cancer: How My Faith Journey Made Me Whole*, tells the manifestation of God's healing power being showcased in one's life by the supernatural disappearing of a critical condition diagnosed by man.

This faith-filled book will empower, encourage and equip any individual to embrace the promises of God. This book brings forward the true essence of a life of faith that becomes synergized with prophetic promises.

Griffin's book captures the power of testimony and illuminates the Glory of God. Jeremiah 30:17 makes mention that God would restore health to us and heal our wounds. Alicia's faith journey has brought her to the destination of health and healing. She is now living the reality of a Prophetic Word.

Prophet Jolando D. Butler
Founder, Jolando Butler Ministries, Alabama

The Scriptures declare in Revelation 12:11 KJV that, "...they overcame him by the blood of the Lamb, and by the word of their testimony; and they loved not their lives unto the death." Rarely do you find someone who truly becomes the epitome and embodiment of this scripture, in such a manner that they may truly be a blessing to others. Minister Alicia Griffin's testimony of God's supernatural healing power will be used by God as a conduit for miraculous healings in the lives of countless individuals around the globe. Diagnosis: Cancer: How My Faith Journey Made Me Whole is a must read for anyone who is challenged with any form of sickness.

Apostle L.M. and Prophetess Valora Cole
Senior Pastor's, Perfected Love International Fellowship
Founders, Coalition Force International

Diagnosis: Cancer

Diagnosis: Cancer

Table of Contents

Diagnosis: Cancer

Foreword

With great intent, God purposefully and intentionally places people on our paths. On this faith journey, their position may seem insignificant, but understandably, there is an underlying predestined wealth of provisions waiting to be unveiled and claimed. Some encounters may last for a moment; whereas, other moments may lead to a season or a lifetime. Despite the length in time, there is one thing I presume: "They come for a specific assignment or for a specific purpose." It is often through these divine connections that God reveals His amazing power to strategically set in motion our passage to the next level. I truly believe "we go from faith to faith, and from level to level". With purpose and intent, this is what The Lord did through my relationship with Alicia.

I have served as the Senior Pastor of Mount Olive Baptist Church (MOBC) for the past twelve years. During this time, I have met many wonderful people through the Lord's supernatural aide, one being Alicia. Alicia's entrance into our spiritual family was essential, and she arrived during a pivotal time in our ministry. We were in transition. We had just built our new church, The Family Life Center, and we were searching for souls to fill the building and community partnerships to assist in our discipleship. Alicia's passion for life, zeal, spiritual insight, and immeasurable faith were relished assets at MOBC, and we welcomed her. Together, we launched our first Back-to-School-Bash. With the success of this community outreach, I knew her visit to MOBC was predestined, and I begin to recognize the provisions God had sent our way through her.

Diagnosis: Cancer

As a pastor and counselor, with over twenty years of experience in ministry, I have witnessed many demonic attacks in the lives of God's people. With my knowledge and my wife's skill as a registered nurse, we have used our professional expertise and spiritual insight to help the people of God and ourselves. In particular, we've used our arsenal of spiritual insight and experience to battle cancer.

One day I remember Alicia and her husband coming to the altar for prayer. The Lord said to me " tell her I will be with her through this journey, she will not be alone." In my spirit, I knew, she would have to go through this process, but she would live and not die. Often, God, through His sovereign wisdom, chooses to take our faith on a journey. It is through this journey of faith God develops and shapes us into our predestined purpose. It was as if the Lord chose to use her life as a sacrifice of what He can do with resilient faith. I recall Jesus telling Simon Peter, "Satan desires to have you that he may sift you like wheat, but I have prayed for you that your faith fail not" (Lk.22:31,32).

Like many of you who may be reading this book, many of our members have been directly or indirectly affected by this deadly disease. The fight against cancer is freighting, painful, and unpredictable. It is a place of constant fear, ongoing physical pain, and an array of unallied challenges. During these times, our faith in God must rise beyond Mt. Evert's peak to a level of security and assurance. While reading this book, you will discover your innate power as a believer to put your faith in action.

Foreword

While dealing with this disease, we have learned the art of spiritual warfare and the power of prayer. This book gives us vivid details and candid experiences of the author's spiritual warfare and how she overcame and defeated cancer. As you continue reading, you will witness many battles, struggles, and fights that appear to be natural manifestations, but truly they are demonically influenced and must be dealt with in the spirit realm. As a spiritual leader and advisor, I believe with all my heart this book will give many individual and families the spiritual insight needed to overcome this deadly disease. If you are battling for your life, for your family, or a friend, this book is for you. It is a must read! It has the power to change your life and equip you with the knowledge and tools you need to gain victory over any demonic attack you are encountering. It's filled with real life experiences, and it offers revelations and strategies to help overcome spiritual attacks from the enemy.

In this book you will discover ways to overcome negative feelings, negative thoughts and even negative words spoken over your life. As you read, you will discover that overcoming negative emotions was a key to her victory. In detail, she candidly describes the stages of emotional and spiritual attacks: shock, blame, fear, depression and loneliness. Despite the underlying origin, we all can identify with these emotions. God has given Alicia, through her journey of faith, a revelation of understanding to recognize we don't have to succumb to any attack of the enemy, despite its pretentions.

Personally, this book is one of the most insightful, empowering, and life changing books I have ever read. It confirms many messages I have ministered on spiritual warfare.

You have heard it said time and time again that your attitude determines your altitude. How true this statement really is can be mind blowing. Alicia's fight to overcome this deadly disease brings this statement alive. Sometimes, we are too quick to accept unwarranted circumstances as God's will for our lives, but what if it's not his will? What if it's His will for you to live and not die? What if it's His will for you to fight for your life? What if it's His will for you to overcome cancer? The transformation begins with your mind. God says, "My people are destroyed for a lack of knowledge" (Hosea 4:6). Are you up for the challenge? Are you prepared to be a change agent for your own mind? We'll let's get started. Beloved, the journey is about to begin.

Sincerely,

Pastor James E. Griffin

Preface

I will kill you with cancer!

It was that chilly, evil whisper from my past again. I felt cold though it was a beautiful, balmy day. We were driving south on Interstate seventy-five headed to Miami Pier. My husband, Terrence, was driving. Our children and a few of their friends were in the back of the truck laughing and having a great time.

I sat beside Terrence as I looked out of the window. I was not there. I was in a dark, lonely place tormented by a voice from the past.

I rebuke you, Satan!

My mind kept going back and forth between the memory of that evil voice and the phone conversation I had with my God-sister Ericka.

She wanted to know if I had received the call from the physician regarding my blood work. I told her yes and that they said that my hemoglobin level was 7.5. She immediately got upset and stated that my blood level was really low and there was a possibility that I would need a blood transfusion.

I had been experiencing daily, increasing presence of blood in my stool. I promised her that once I returned from my cruise with the family, I would immediately admit myself into a medical facility.

Diagnosis: Cancer

Meanwhile, spring break is here. I am on a cruise with all my loved ones around me. Is this the last spring break I would ever experience? I plastered a smile and pretended to have a good time, but in that dark place in my mind, the raging torrent of thoughts would not let up.

What is wrong? Why me? Will I live? Is there hope?

That distant refrain persisted; I will kill you with cancer. I will kill you with cancer...

That marked the beginning of a journey. Through medication, meditation on the LORD and memorializing my experiences in copious daily journals, I battled one of the deadliest diseases known – colorectal cancer. You are about to join me on a journey of tragedies that ended up in triumphs as the LORD struck me with a total and debilitating blindness. Yes, blindness to my circumstance. But then, He became my Guide. He gave me twenty-twenty spiritual vision as I wore my night-vision goggles of faith to walk through the dark valley of the shadow of death.

By faith, I saw not the circumstances, but the LORD above the circumstances as I held onto the prophetic promise that was spoken over my life by Prophet Jolando Butler months prior to the illness.

I slowly but surely learned the law of faith in the Most High God. He walked with me, and so will He walk with you. Will you take His hand and join us in this faith journey toward destiny?

CHAPTER ONE

WARNING SIGNALS

What more could a lady ask for? We had just relocated to Alabama with my new husband, Terrence Griffin, and our children, Jasmine and TerQuan. I was enjoying newly wedded bliss with the love of my life, setting up home and hearth and looking for things to do in my new environment.

Very soon, I became acquainted with the locals, found a wonderful church family where I was welcomed and attended regular fellowship. Soon, I set up a financial business and started the first community newspaper, SE Bama Entertainer.

Our children quickly settled into their school, meeting new friends, and adjusting to the slower pace of small-city life. Furthermore, I became closely acquainted with a few sisters in the church and a few employees that I had hired in my businesses.

Once the newspaper went into circulation, I started First Friday Networking Group where local business owners met for networking purposes. I would choose to highlight a business owner for the month. On his assigned particular month, the business owner would speak about his business and the services he offers.

During our second meeting, a business that promotes a machine that can tell whether your blood levels are normal by simply placing your hand on top of it came to make a presentation to the group.

Diagnosis: Cancer

All my employees were given an opportunity to have their levels tested with that method and they seemed fine. When my turn came, I placed my hand on the machine and waited.

The young lady who was conducting the test looked at her assistant and then at me and said, "How do you feel?" I stated that I felt fine. She told me that according to the machine that measured my levels, it seemed that something was wrong. She advised me that out of 76 levels 61 of mine were not leveled. I told her that it had to be incorrect because there was nothing wrong with me. I was not over or under weight or ill.

She performed the same test on the other people present in the meeting and everyone's results seemed fine, except mine. I looked at Terrence who was there with me and said, "I don't know what's wrong with that machine. How can everyone here be fine except me? Besides, I am not sick, I'm perfectly healthy."

When I got home that night, all I could think was, "What is wrong with me?"

At the time, I had not mentioned to Terrence that I had experienced blood in my stool intermittently over the years and that it had gotten worse recently. I had always been told that it was just a small case of hemorrhoids; only, it had become worse.

Ever since that night at the First Friday Networking, the words of that young lady stayed in my mind, Are you feeling okay? There is something wrong. You need to get yourself checked.

The increasing amount of blood in my stool did not make me feel any better.

Spiritual Attacks

Before I get into spiritual attacks, I would like to explain one thing: In Christianity, we understand that there is a very real spiritual world which influences the things that happen in our physical world.

The Bible says in Ephesians 6:12, NLT:

For we are not fighting against flesh-and-blood enemies, but against evil rulers and authorities of the unseen world, against mighty powers in this dark world, and against evil spirits in the heavenly places.

There is the kingdom of God from where all that is good and life-giving stems, and there is the kingdom of darkness under the devil which opposes all that is good from the LORD. Every person who has been on this earth is a target for the kingdom of darkness to destroy in their bid to resist the purposes of the LORD.

Why? First, every human being is created in the image and likeness of God, whether they choose to believe it or not. Therefore, when the enemy sees you, he sees the image and likeness of his greatest enemy that is the LORD God.

Second, the only vessel that can fulfill the purposes of God is mankind. We have the free will to choose whether we will serve God and fulfill His purposes or serve the kingdom of darkness and thwart the LORD's desires. When we do not actively make the choice to serve the LORD, we are free agents that can be used by the kingdom of darkness to do wickedness with or without our own knowledge.

Some of the things people call imaginary or paranormal in science, are simply spiritual things.

Jesus Christ revealed that sickness and diseases are caused by demonic spirits which are under the control of the devil. However, when they are rebuked in faith, they leave the victim and the person afflicted becomes whole again.

Years prior to that scenario, I would get tormenting verbal attacks from demonic spirits. In those times, I would hear these spirits say, "I will kill you with cancer." I never knew why those vicious words kept coming at me. Whenever that happens, I would rebuke those spirits and command them to be silent. Then, I would cancel those words and declare, "The devil is a liar."

Part of the voluntary service I offered to the church was to assist the pastor's wife. We referred to that role as armor bearer. When the verbal attacks became frequent, I told my pastor's wife about them. She advised me to pray and cancel out those ill-spoken words from the kingdom of darkness. She said that she had done the same thing in those times in her life when the demons also told her that they would kill her.

Because of what the young lady had told me, the presence of blood in my stool, the memory of those evil words began to return. I knew something was wrong. I did some internet research about internal intestinal bleeding. In every
search, it said that if I had blood in my stool, it was one of two

4

things: either it was hemorrhoids or it was colon or rectal cancer.

I began to feel anxious.

Getting Worse

Surely it had to be a bad case of hemorrhoids. I couldn't possibly have cancer. Yet at the back of my mind, I just knew something was seriously wrong.

Soon, I began to tire easily and was constantly weak. I knew I was slightly anemic because of the continued blood loss. I tried to take supplements and eat healthy to help the situation. I had not felt the need to see a doctor for my condition yet. Truth is I do not like hospitals and the smell of antiseptics. Moreover, I am terrified of needles so I avoided any hospital encounters as much as possible.

The blood loss increased daily and its color tuned into bright red. I called my God-sister Ericka, a registered nurse, to tell her about the appearance of bright red blood and she informed me that I was actively bleeding internally.

Then, it got to a point that when I went to the bathroom, the toilet bowl would be full of blood. That's how bad it had become and it started to scare me. One day, Terrence came into the bathroom and was shocked to see the amount of blood. It was he who urged me to visit a physician.

Diagnosis: Cancer

CHAPTER TWO

MEDICAL CHECK-UPS

At Terrence's urging, I decided to make an appointment with the local physician's office. It was a medical center that my friend, Brenda, had been attending for years and she escorted me there.

When I got in, the nurse took my vitals and reported that everything was fine. I went in to see the doctor and told him my symptoms. He told me that it had to be hemorrhoids and not cancer. Colon cancer is normally diagnosed in mostly male patients from fifty years old and up. And by just looking at me, he ruled out the possibility of colon cancer.

I was thirty-nine years old and in good health; my weight was within the recommended levels for my height. My vitals were fine and I did not have any adverse conditions.

He said, "You are not obese. Most people in these towns are obese. They don't care how they eat so they have all these health problems." He pointed out that he would get my blood count and would have the nurse call me for the results within three days.

I know I should have felt assured of my well-being when I left the doctor's office. Besides, that doctor stated that there was no way I could have cancer, right? Yet somehow, I instinctively knew that something was just not right.

I let the whole issue rest because we had a full schedule of activities ahead. I needed to be focused. The children were all excited because spring break was coming, and we had this big cruise planned for of them and some of their friends.

The day came and we set off on the long drive from Alabama heading all the way down to the docking pier in Miami.

Diagnosis: Cancer

You can imagine the excitement in our children, and the level of happy noises inside the vehicle. I was preoccupied for most of the ride. All I could do was wonder, *why am I losing so much blood? Why do I feel so weak and tired on a daily basis?*

I will kill you with cancer!

It was that chilly, evil whisper from my past again. I felt cold though it was a beautiful, balmy day. We were driving south on Interstate Seventy Five headed to Miami Pier. Terrence was driving and I struggled to engage in the general small talk in the vehicle, but I was not there. I was in a dark, lonely place tormented by a voice from the past.

I rebuke you, Satan!

As soon as we arrived on Alligator Alley, Ericka called to find out if I had received the call from the physician regarding my blood work. My mind kept going back and forth between the memory of that evil voice and the phone conversation I had with Ericka.

I had told her yes and that the nurse from the physician's office had called and said that my hemoglobin level was 7.5. Ericka immediately got upset and stated that my blood level was really low and there was a possibility that I would need blood transfusion.

I told Ericka that I had travelled on advice. I had asked the nurse if it was okay for me to go on this cruise we had pre-planned. She had said it would be fine if, as soon as I got home, I

Would go and get iron supplements. Also, she advised me to eat plenty of nutritious fruits and vegetables.

Ericka persisted, "Alicia, do you know how serious this is?" She was arguing about the wisdom of going on this cruise. We were an hour and a half from arriving at our destination. She made me promise that I would admit myself into a medical facility immediately when we get back.

I assured her that once I returned from my vacation with the family, I would at once do as she had advised. With such anxiety coming from my own God-sister who was a registered nurse, it began to bother me that I was in much worse condition than what I actually felt.

Diagnosis: Cancer

The Cruise

Meanwhile, spring break has arrived and I was on a cruise with all my loved ones around me. Is this the last spring break I would ever experience? I plastered a smile, pretended to have a good time but in that dark place in my mind, the raging torrent of thoughts would not let up.

What is wrong? Why me? Will I live? Is there hope?

That distant refrain persisted; *I will kill you with cancer. I Will kill you with cancer...*

The cruise was a memorable experience for everyone. We had a wonderful, restful time in the boat. I did a lot of resting and plenty of vegetables and fruit eating the entire time I was on the cruise. I knew I must fortify my body and prepare my mind for the hated hospital admission. At the back of my mind, I sensed that there is a great possibility that I had some sort of Cancer.

Terrence and I had beautiful times together on the boat. Even so, there would be moments when I told him that I was going up on the deck to get some sun. I wanted to be alone, so, I would lie out there, look up into the sky, and speak to the LORD.

During those times I would say, "God, I don't know what is going on but Your Hand is upon me. Please guide me. Direct my paths, O LORD. I don't know what is going to happen. Guide me. Hold my hand. I know You Are with me. Grace and mercy follow me all the days of my life. I do not know what journey I am about to embark on but walk with me."

I would watch the teens having so much fun with their whole lives ahead of them, and would begin to think, *LORD, in this time next year, allow me to see my daughter. My baby girl is getting ready to graduate in two years, LORD. All I ask is that I can watch her walk across the stage to graduate.*

Our days in the sun and sea were beautiful, but as soon as the boat began to dock, the spirit of fear began to crawl inside me. I hated hospitals and the deep fear of needles was back with a vengeance.

Diagnosis: Cancer

Second Check-Up

When we arrived in Cape Coral outside of my home town in Fort Myers where my mom and sisters reside, I spoke to Ericka and she suggested that I get checked into the hospital where she was working.

I went into the room and laid across the bed. All the while, I was dreading the hospital visit I knew I had to get done right away. And so, after a few hours, I finally got up and went to Lee Memorial Hospital. I arrived at the Emergency Room and told staff about my condition.

When I completed my Internet research and figured that there was a possibility I might have colon cancer, I knew I would have to get a colonoscopy. At the time, I did not have medical insurance. I knew if I went to hospital and my blood level is low because I was losing blood, they would admit me and offer a colonoscopy.

That did not happen. The medical staff took such good care of me and to my surprise, the doctor came and stated that my blood levels had come up and I do not need blood transfusion. Hallelujah!

Ericka said that it had to be the LORD's doing.

Overjoyed that I did not have to get a blood transfusion and I could go home, I planned a big party. It was the day before my mom's birthday. Somehow the thought came, What if I am not here next year? I want her to have the best birthday ever.

So, we stayed in Fort Myers and threw my mom a nice surprise birthday party. It was the first time that everyone was There including her children, grandchildren and some of my in-

Laws. As I sat there looking at everyone having a good time, all I could think of was, *I am going to enjoy the moment. I am going to enjoy the moment...*

As the day wore on, I found myself getting sad as I looked around at all these people whom I love deeply, have such a blissful time together. My mom and the other members of our extended family were a having a great time while my thoughts run: *Maybe, I will not be around to see them enter their first day of school. I will not be able to enjoy another spontaneous fun-time like this. My husband would be a widower? Who would guide my girls for me?*

I would get overwhelmed and would go to the bathroom to weep a little. Of course, I could not let anyone see me cry. I thought to myself: *My mom is so happy because everyone is here to celebrate her birthday. She does not know what the coming days have in store for her eldest child.*

The day came to an end and our visit in Fort Myers with it. We were ready for our journey back home. As we travelled on the road back to Alabama, all I could think of was, As soon as I get home, I would do further research on these symptoms.

In my mind, the battle with that evil voice persisting that I would die continued. Was the enemy right? My mind was filled with morbid thoughts of death. Am I dying?

I would not see my daughter graduate from high school. I was newlywed and the thought of leaving my beloved Terrence to be a widower so soon after our union is simply heart-breaking. That was the longest drive back home ever.

Diagnosis: Cancer

CHAPTER THREE

DIAGNOSIS: CANCER!

We returned to Alabama and everyone was settled into the new school and work season. The symptoms were getting worse and I knew my blood count had to be decreasing. It was only a matter of time before I would need blood transfusion and that was something that I did not want.

The dreaded doctor visit was upon me. When I went to see him, he told me to just eat plenty of green vegetables because I looked perfectly healthy. I told him my concerns regarding colon cancer. Yet again, he stated that I did not have to worry about that. Besides, I was too young.

When I left the doctor's office, my spirit was not at ease. I knew I had to get a colonoscopy done just for peace's sake.

I called several other doctors' offices to try and schedule a colonoscopy. Most of them would not set an appointment with me stating that I needed a referral, or that I wasn't due for one yet. I had called over twenty-three doctors before I finally got someone who was willing to make an appointment with me. The doctor's appointment was on a Monday.

By the time I got the colonoscopy appointment, I had not been approved for medical insurance, so I expected to pay directly for the treatment. I had put all of those issues before the LORD in prayer.

That weekend before I went into hospital, I attended a prayer conference which we refer to as *revival meeting*. In those

meetings, the speakers taught on different biblical topics that
dealt with various areas of life. They also prayed over people.
There were also prophets who foretold various occurrences in
people's personal lives. There was a lot of encouragement to have
faith in the LORD and to live in peace with all people. I prayed
throughout that weekend asking the LORD to stand by me as I
undergo the colonoscopy.

In all the revival meetings that weekend, it was as if
someone had singled me out to receive prophetic words from the
prophets who came to speak. I was the only one they would
point out to with a word of encouragement like:

"You will sit among kings and queens."
"I see an angel with his foot on your rooftop saying,
'Victory!'"
"The LORD favors you."

The prophets, whom I had not known before, spoke
those and many other encouraging words to me. That made me
aware that I had a battle coming. In His providence, the LORD
was letting me know the good end of the encounter so that no
matter what I experienced in the coming season, I would hold on
to those words of encouragement and promise.

Divine Providence

When God gives you prophecies or promises, understand
that it is because you will need the encouragement from those
promises when things become very difficult. Those wonderful
words that give you goose-bumps and let you feel the sweet, real
presence of the LORD proves that hard times will come. And

when they do, you will feel as though He has abandoned you and you will probably question your choices.

But it is in those difficult times that I went back to the LORD and lay hold of His promise – *God, didn't you say you will do the ABCD?*

Every time God gives me a seemingly great promise, I believe that it is His message that He Who sees into the future saw the possibility that I will divert from the course because of the various difficult circumstances that are coming to me. So, He was basically saying, "If you will stay on course, then, I will reward you this way."

He did that for me to understand that when the time came and circumstances began to draw me away from the LORD, I would have motivation and determination in my life to stay on course. At that point, I could lay hold of His promise and say, "But LORD, You said this so I will stick to your course."

That was the purpose of those numerous words of prophecy spoken over my life before I even went for the colonoscopy.

When God says anything like that, it means in His providence, in His foresight, He sees you as an overcomer. He wants to say to you, "I will be there to help you if you will choose to stay on course with me through the rough patch ahead. I have already provided your way out."

Nothing catches the LORD by surprise. He does not wave His hands saying, "O dear, now the devil has stricken Alicia with that illness. What shall we do?" He who sees every plan of the enemy has given provision to counter it, if we CHOOSE to take His course.

The LORD says, *"For I know the plans I have for you...plans of good and not of evil, to give you a good end"* (Jeremiah 29:11).

17

God's providence infers that every detail in creation, whether it is good or bad, **can be brought under the control of God if we choose** to submit it to Him. For instance, Jesus told Pilate in John 19:11:

```
You would have no power over me, if it were
not given to you from above.
```

In other words, because Jesus Christ had chosen the LORD's will – "not as I will but as you will" (Matthew 26:39), Pilate could not do anything in that circumstance except that which was allowed by God's providence. Jesus had been walking in the will of God even when it seemed that evil circumstances were coming at Him. He knew that it was God's hand at work.

Even when we fall in sin, God is aware and has made a way out for us in that circumstance. It is up to us to choose whether we will stay within God's course or not.

God has foresight. He saw the end of my ordeal from the beginning and saw where the traps were. Then He said, "Knowing your heart, you will be weak at this point. You will be tempted and you will feel a great pull to turn away, but I Am not at a loss in these situations."

"I am telling you, I have sent an angel to fight for you and when he is done, he will be on your rooftop proclaiming victory. I have given you favor. I will bring you to sit before kings and queens."

"In every circumstance that you may find yourself into, I can do something about it. So I say to you, if at that moment you will choose to stay with Me, this is what I will do to you. If you choose not to stay with Me, this is what will happen."

Diagnosis: Cancer

When you reach that point, whatever happens is not news to God. He knows the consequence of your every choice and has provided a way of escape for you. If you lose the balance of personal responsibility – the choices you will make in each situation – you will end up being complacent and just letting things happen.

The fact that God makes promises to you very clearly about a situation you are to embark on, proves that difficult times will come in your life where you will question your choices. So in those times, you can go back to God and lay hold of what He had said or showed you at the beginning.

Many people claim that God spoke to them concerning various endeavors in their lives. But when they hit the hard rocks in their journey, they abandon ship. The common declaration is, "God has given me another direction." Some would simply doubt if God had really spoken at all. They thought those prophetic words were uttered for that feel-good moment. Yet, God's word must fulfill what He wants it to accomplish. He must do what He said He will do.

It is not so much that God did not speak. He knew the great testing and temptations you would face in the future. In His PROVIDENCE, He saw it fit to show you the expected end in a supernatural way – through a dream, a vision, or in my case, through prophecies.

That expected end becomes your motivation to push through the challenges and stay on course. Today, learn that when you hear those words of promise, let the warning go deep and be watchful of the tough times ahead.

Third Medical Check-up

On the same day that I got the confirmation for my colonoscopy, I received the approval for my medical insurance.

Diagnosis: Cancer

That was an answer to my prayer; that was another sign of the LORD's favor in my life.

The weekend was over and Monday, May 10, 2010, finally arrived. That trip to the physician's office marked the first of my countless hospital trips to come.

Terrence was with me. And as I sat in the waiting room, all I could see around me were much older patients. I asked, "God, what am I doing here?"

My turn came, so I went in and told the doctor about the blood in my stool. He had the nurse take my vitals and prepare me for sedation before the procedure. While she was talking to me during the procedure, all I could think of was: *LORD please let everything be all right.*

They colonoscopy was performed. I remembered that when I was coming out of sedation, I looked up and saw a lady, in all white, standing beside the bed. I called out to her, "Brenda." I thought my friend had come to be with me during the procedure. The lady said to me, "I am not Brenda. I am your guardian angel." When I was fully conscious, I saw my husband and asked him where Brenda was. He said that Brenda was not there. He thought I was still under sedation, so, I told him about the angel.

When the doctor came in, he told us that there was a tumor in my colon. I asked him whether he had removed it. He stated that it was too big, about eight centimeters in diameter. He had to send it off for a biopsy to check if it was cancerous. The results would come within three to five days.

It was at that moment that I sensed it was cancerous. I Figured that is probably the reason God sent me a guardian angel. It was an assurance that He was watching over me throughout the procedure.

We left for home and I waited for those really long two days. I called on Thursday for the results but was told that it was not in yet. When I called that Friday, the nurse asked for my name and security question. When I told her that I was calling for the biopsy results, she put me on hold and was gone for quite a long time. When she got back, the tone in her voice had changed. She was abrupt and would not give me the results over the phone. All she told me was, "We need you here at ten o'clock on Monday." I agreed.

I thought I had experienced excruciatingly long days Before. However, that weekend had to be the longest ever. At that time, all I could do was pray and remind the LORD of all the promises He had given me.

Terrence was a real trooper. He was my pillar during that weekend. He was very positive and told me that I was probably over-reacting to the way the nurse had spoken. However, I told him that the way she was over the phone and the tone of her voice were as good as telling me what was wrong with the results.

We had been praying that it would be anything but Cancer. I told the LORD, "Take this cup from me. I do not want to go through this."

We went for my appointment that Monday. I sat on the examination table while Terrence sat on the chair. When the doctor came in, he looked at my hands and ordered me to open my mouth. He then asked me how I was feeling. I said I was very fine.

Then, he told us that my biopsy results showed that the tumor was cancerous. I could not say anything. I just nodded my

Diagnosis: Cancer

Head and looked over at my husband. We both were totally stunned. The doctor stated that he was going to refer me to the one of the best surgeons and colon cancer specialist in the country.

This cannot be happening. I just got married a little over a year. I am just getting settled in a new state, with a new business. Everything is going good. I'm loving my new church family and pastors. How can this be happening? What about my husband and children? Would I be able to see our grandchildren grow up? Was the enemy right? Would I really die of cancer?

All these things were running through my head.

Terrence and I silently went to the waiting room. I could not say a word. I was just thinking, *God, why me? What have I done?* Then, I started repenting, *LORD, please forgive me for anything I have done to make this come upon me.*

Terrence was equally quiet. I wondered what was going through his mind. I wanted to ask, yet, I could not speak. Immediately, I began to think of death. *I was going to die. My husband would be a widower. I would not see my children graduate. How long do I have? What are the things I need to prepare for my departure?*

Then the doctor came back to see us. He tried to assure us that everything would be fine and that people do survive from cancer. The medical technology had improved and not everybody die from cancer.

At that point, it hit me.

I've just been diagnosed with Cancer!

CHAPTER FOUR

THE FEAR FACTOR

We left the doctor's office.

We got into the truck. Terrence was still silent. I know my husband is a very calm man. He was thinking, too. I guess he was wondering: *She has been going to the revival meetings almost every night and this is what God has allowed to happen to her?*

It was surprising for me to be so terribly shaken at the results of the biopsy even though I had that subconscious knowledge that I have something worse than hemorrhoids. Coupled with all the symptoms and the prophecies that had gone before, I sensed that I was in an awful condition. Still, the thought that I have cancer paralyzed me. I don't know how much worse the fear could have been had I not been pre-empted by the LORD.

Throughout the weeks when my suspicions about Having something worse than hemorrhoids had not yet been confirmed, I had not experienced that level of fear. I just knew that the LORD was in control. But somewhere in the days after I had been diagnosed with cancer, I felt that God's hedge of protection around me had somehow been broken down. I felt exposed, vulnerable and utterly fearful. Even as I prayed, I could not dislodge this fear.

I had a voice embedded inside me that was saying, "I Know what you are going to experience. Remember what I spoke to you. Remember the prophetic promises."

23

Diagnosis: Cancer

Why? Fear had been lodged within me and with it came thoughts of death and destruction. The door had been opened somewhere; therefore, I began to think back to where it could have happened.

I realized that it started on that day when I called the doctor's office to ask about the results. The nurse's tone of voice told me something was very wrong even though she would not specifically say what it was. I figured that when she got my results, she panicked or got fearful. She did not know how to deliver the message without actually saying that I have cancer. She had put me on hold for a long time, then came back on the phone, put me on hold again, and by the time she was telling me to come in the following Monday, she could hardly communicate. That's when the spirit of fear crept in. Looking back, I learned a very important lesson concerning fear.

Fear is highly contagious. The nurse opened the door to Fear and when I heard it from her, it entered into me. I had not anticipated her fearful response; therefore, I was somewhat open to whatever emotions she would transmit as she spoke to me. The Bible says in Ephesians 6:13, 16, KJV 2000:

```
Therefore take unto you the whole armor of
God, that you may be able to withstand in
the evil day, and having done all, to stand
[...] Above all,    taking   the   shield   of
faith, with which you shall be able to
quench all the fiery darts of the wicked
one.
                                --EMPHASIS ADDED
```

Fear creeps in when faith is absent.

The Fear Factor

Whenever I receive prophetic promises or at whatever time I pray, I have increased faith. My focus is on the LORD Who Is above all challenges of life. I did not look at the circumstances around me, no matter how fearful they seemed to be. However, in one unguarded moment, someone opened a door to fear and I was ensnared because my shield of faith was not up.

Words are powerful. The words we receive will either make or break us. I realized how important it is to command faith each day so that each word that will come from and to me will be aimed at building and not destroying someone or something.

Furthermore, it is important to raise the shield of faith and take captive every word, every thought that people have towards you. I appreciate Psalm 141:3 where the psalmist made an important prayer:

Set a guard over my mouth, LORD; keep watch over the door of my lips.

Isaiah 50:4 further said:

The Sovereign LORD has given me a well-instructed tongue, to know the word that sustains the weary.

Thoughts are projected too. The nurse did not really say anything, but her thoughts were full of fear and they infected me.

How do you stop a scenario like the one I experienced from happening? I learned the importance of praying for medical personnel. I learned to raise the shield of faith before I start communicating with them.

Diagnosis: Cancer

As I prepare for each day, I pray that the shield of faith would deflect and quench any fiery darts of fear, uncertainty, or anything that would shake my faith in whatever task I would embark on. Moreover, I pray that people's negative words or thoughts would not affect me and that I would take control of my spiritual space by shielding myself with faith in God for every circumstance, more so, when I experience trials and temptations. The Bible says in 2 Corinthians 10:3-6:

For though we walk in the flesh, we do not war according to the flesh: (For the weapons of our warfare are not carnal, but mighty through God to the pulling down of strongholds ;) Casting down arguments, and every high thing that exalts itself against the knowledge of God, and bringing into captivity every thought to the obedience of Christ.

—EMPHASIS ADDED

You can capture every negative thought projected towards you or your situation and bring it into obedience to the LORD Jesus Christ. This is a very deep, important but often neglected factor. Imaginations and thoughts can be projected.

Sometimes, after speaking with someone, you suddenly begin to feel anxious. It is because he may have passed on his anxiety to you.

When I realized that, I began to repent for opening the door to fear. I reminded myself of the LORD's promises Concerning my life. I began to encourage myself in the LORD.

The Fear Factor

If He had so clearly shown me that He was with me, then, everything would be all right. He is a Great God, the Great King above all gods. He is Jehovah Rappha – the LORD my Healer.

Because of fear, I began to take His thoughts about me – what He said in the Scriptures about me; what He said to me through His promises – and replaced them with thoughts of destruction and death.

If the LORD had found it extremely significant to experience the breaking of His body so that we would specifically experience peace and healing, then, I could lay hold of that promise that His chastisement was for my peace and His stripes were for my healing. The Bible says:

```
But He was wounded for our transgressions;
He was bruised for our iniquities: the
chastisement of our peace was upon Him; and
with His stripes we are healed.
```

—ISAIAH 53:6

My faith began to rise again. I was encouraged in my spirit but I could not say the same for my husband. I could not say the same for my family to whom I had yet to break the news. I did not know how they would react.

When we got home, I called Ericka and gave her the news; she broke down. She was nearly hysterical while saying that she would travel with her pastor to Alabama to be with me. In all that, I remained very calm and strong in faith. I had already learned my lesson and had raised the shield of faith to deflect any ill-spoken word concerning my condition. Ericka kept asking me, "Do you not realize what you have? You are not taking it seriously. You have a deadly disease."

Diagnosis: Cancer

I could understand where she was coming from. She was a registered nurse and had obviously been acquainted with various forms of cancer. She knew what she was talking about when she made those statements because she was looking at it from a scientific and experiential perspective.

Nevertheless, I had a higher view. As she spoke, I felt my Faith rise in me and I told her, "No, do you NOT realize what God I serve?" When her pastor heard what I had told her, she said to her, "We are not going. If she has faith, then that is all that matters."

My position in the LORD was exceedingly high above any name that can be named. Cancer is just a name. The Bible says in Ephesians 1:19b-21; 2:6, NASB:

These are in accordance with the working of the strength of His [God's] might which He brought about in Christ, **when He raised Him from the dead and seated Him at His [God's] right hand in the heavenly places, far above all rule and authority and power and dominion, and every name that is named,** not only in this age but also in the age to come [...] and raised us up with Him, and seated us with Him in the heavenly places in Christ Jesus.

—EMPHASIS ADDED

It was the understanding of my position in the LORD – that lofty place seated with Christ in God far above every name

28

that could be named – that made me declare my statements of faith. Cancer was just a name.

From that time on, I never heard a negative word from her any more. I proclaimed that by the stripes of Jesus Christ, I was healed.

Notice the difference in the way I was able to deal with my God-sister's fear and infect her with my faith as compared to the way the nurse infected me with fear. If not for the knowledge that the LORD is on my side and the truth of my position in Him, I would not have risen to counter those negative impressions of fear that had come against me.

Every negative emotion feeds the enemy of your soul. It energizes him to destroy you further. Any positive emotion energizes your spirit. It will enable you to resist the enemy and make something happen no matter how difficult your circumstances are.

Never fear. Have faith.

Diagnosis: Cancer

CHAPTER FIVE

FAITH

When fear knocks and faith opens the door, he (faith) will find no one.

When you speak a word of faith, fear can't help but leave because faith and fear cannot dwell in the same room. The nurse at the doctor's office infected me with fear, but I was able to counter it with my faith statements until it was completely eradicated.

When I told my God-sister about the doctor's diagnosis, she flipped out. But when I declared my statements of faith regarding my condition, Ericka was infected with faith.

She is a nurse and from her experience, she knew what this illness is capable of doing to its victim and family. It was crumbling. Yet, my statements of faith turned her around.

Cancer treatment is a long-drawn-out affair. You need to have staying power to survive this ordeal. That staying power comes from standing in faith. You cannot psyche yourself into that position. You must actively pray, continuously prophesy, and speak to your *mountain about* your God who created that *mountain.* **Command it to move.**

Jesus Christ said that if you have faith, you can speak to the mountain and it shall move and be cast into the sea (Matthew 17:20, 21:21; Mark 11:23). Most of the time, we come to the LORD to talk to Him about our mountains, yet, He has given us all we need for life and godliness (2 Peter 1:3-4). We normally come to the LORD with our challenges and tell Him all about our trials and how we suffer greatly from them. Then, we finish with a plea asking the LORD to come into the situation and clear it out for us. But then, God looks down at us and tells, "But I have already given the answer to all your troubles. I gave you your healing for more than two thousand years ago. Take it and work out your salvation. Walk in faith; speak in faith to that virus, that tumor or that name and command it to leave your body."

When you reach that point in your life, the LORD will then prescribe your particular treatment. The topic *Jesus Heals Diversely* is expounded on Appendix II.

Blinding Faith

In these kinds of situations, you can easily get struck by blinding faith. I mentioned in the preface that the LORD struck me with blindness to my temporal physical circumstance so that He could become my Guide.

He began to teach me to perceive permanent spiritual realities based on what He was verbalizing – His Rhema. The NOW words concerning my life.

He already said that I was healed and I have the victory. I am going to walk in that truth no matter what the medical report had said or what the treatment would do to me. After coming from the doctor's office, I knew I had to make that decision: To walk in blind faith.

Blind faith became my strong foundation for the rough Times ahead. It became my pole star when I was lost in the stormy sea of doubts, despair, loneliness, uncertainties concerning the future, and real brushes with death. I was blind anyway, so, I really didn't see the gravity of some of the circumstances!

Faith

Why is there a need for God to make you spiritually? blind?

Well, ask yourself this: *What is real to you?*

Is it what you see around you? Is it what you hear?

Is it what your doctor, medical report, body, boss or disciplinary memo told you? Is it what your banker, bank statement or lawyer declares? Or is it the news and economic reports?

What motivates you? What determines your ultimate conviction?

Is it popular opinion, statistics, sentiments or expository researches? Is it the mob mentality of your social circle? Or is it the peer pressure of your so-called friends?

What controls your vision?

Is it your past, experiences, education, skills and abilities? Is it your speech, lineage, race, skin color or culture? Or is it your house, clothing, car or community?

If any of that is your frame of reference to determine what is real in your life, then, you have fallen to an illusion of *reality*. God needs to afflict you with a sudden paralyzing blindness for you to believe what is truthfully real.

He will make you blind from the intimidation and harassment of the circumstances. He will cover your eyes from the glaring proof of sickness, evidence of failure and *accounts of* impossibility. Then, you will be forced to start seeing true reality with the eyes of your spirit instead. By that, you will learn to deduce *the facts* from the truth – for only what the TRUTH Himself (John 14:6) says is true. Let God be true and every man a liar (Romans 3:4).

You CANNOT **perceive** spiritual truth with physical senses. Unless you see it, you cannot possess it. I had to see through my spiritual eyes what my healed condition would be like. I began to think of the exploits I was going to do when I had overcome. I began to see myself as an overcomer and not as an invalid.

I planned out my wardrobe for the next season. If and when the treatments begin to affect my appearance, I am going through all of it as a WINNER.

I was not *faking it 'til I made it*, NO. I leaned on the permanent spiritual reality that BY HIS STRIPES, I WAS HEALED and therefore, I walked in that truth and listened obediently to His instruction for my treatment. I was able to achieve that through blinding faith.

The Bible says:

Now faith is the substance of things hoped for, the evidence of things not seen. For by it the elders obtained a good testimony. By faith we understand that the worlds were framed by the word of God, so that the things which are seen were not made of things which are visible [...] But without faith it is impossible to please Him, for he who comes to God must believe that He is, and that He is a Rewarder of those who diligently seek Him.

–HEBREWS 11:1-3, 6

I planned for and took tangible steps of faith concerning the things that I hoped to see happen in my life.

Another source of my faith was my spiritual leaders. They encouraged, prayed and gave me messages that would keep me strong through every trial.

Faith

From Faith to Faith

I got diagnosed in May 2010 when school was almost out. Now that I have cancer, what's next?

My first appointment with Dr. William Taylor made me feel a little better. He explained that I have colorectal cancer and the different stages that come with it. He said that my treatment would depend on how far along the tumor was. Radiation, chemotherapy, or a combination of the two, and then surgery were required to get rid of the tumor. If I have stage four cancer, the last stage, it would be considered as terminal. He said that they would probably find ways to manage it, but there was little that could be done for a terminal cancer.

Dr. Taylor was very informative, yet, he couldn't exactly tell any additional information about my condition. He advised that I need to undergo flex sig procedure.

Flexible sigmoidoscopy (flex sig) is a medical procedure used to see inside the sigmoid colon and rectum. It can detect inflamed tissue, abnormal growths and ulcers. Flex sig is used to look for early signs of cancer and can help doctors diagnose unexplained changes in bowel habits, abdominal pain, bleeding from the anus, and weight loss. Therefore, to determine what is going on in my colon and rectum and to know at what stage the cancerous tumor was in, I was scheduled for a flex sig.

Meanwhile, I got home and prepared to tell my children about my condition. I told my daughter, Jasmine (15), my youngest son, Terquan (13) and my eldest son, Ladarris (17) about the cancer.

They were shocked and saddened. But Ladarris was more courageous than what I had expected. He encouraged and assured me that I would be fine. In turn, I tried to cheer them up by saying that I would be all right.

Diagnosis: Cancer

Nowadays, young people research quite a bit on anything they want to discover. As soon as they were reassured that I was so optimistic about my situation, they were on the internet researching about colorectal cancer.

Jasmine began to tell me, "Mom, you cannot be more than a stage zero to one."

I, as well, had done as much research as I possibly could that pertain to this type of cancer. I had researched the various stages and found that they indeed start from zero to four. My husband would literally pull me away from the computer for I could not stop myself from looking up every informative article about cancer. He felt that it was dragging me daily.

I felt the same as Jasmine, so, I agreed with her.

I was gladdened by my research as all the information I've read showed that stages zero to one do not require chemotherapy. There would only be some radiation therapy but nothing major. I immediately started to pray specifically thanking the LORD that, by faith, I was going to be a stage zero or stage one at worst.

I told my husband and children to remain prayerful. No one else was to know about the condition I was in. This was to be between our family and very close friends.

I called my pastor and his wife to let them know what was going on. First Lady Pamela Griffin was a registered nurse and I had sought her medical advice on several occasions prior to my present condition. As my pastors, family and close friends prayed, I remained calm about the whole thing. It remained for the flex sig to confirm what I had so positively declared in faith concerning the stage of this cancer.

Faith

Once my immediate family stood in faith with me concerning this circumstance, I decided to tell my mom, my sister and God-sisters. I informed them that I would let them know the details once I have the complete information regarding what stage I was in.

My mom was shocked, as any mother would be, to hear that her daughter has cancer. Immediately, she took off from work and came up to be with me in Alabama for two weeks. What she did was a blessing and I thank the LORD for my mother.

Even though it seemed such devastating news for all, I was very strong in faith and encouraged them that with the LORD on our side, we would triumph over this challenge.

The Flex Sig

I went in for the flex sig. They had to sedate me for the procedure. They basically need to examine my rectum and colon using an endoscope. They were going to measure the tumor, determine its stage, and see how much it had spread.

As I was slowly losing consciousness, I prayed and saw my guardian angel for the second time. She was there to reassure me that the LORD was with me. When they had finished the procedure and I was out of sedation, Dr. Taylor told me that the tumor was eight centimeters long and it had spread to three out of four lymph nodes. I told him, "So, you mean it is at stage 3BT1?"

There is only one more level left in stage three before the cancer would have been considered terminal!

Diagnosis: Cancer

He told me that since it was close to terminal, they were going to go at it aggressively. My treatment regimen was going to be very tough physically and mentally.

I was to take twenty-eight rounds of radiation together with daily oral chemotherapy over five weeks. After that, I was to rest for one month to build up my immune system, and then undergo a major surgery. After that surgery, I would go through seven rounds of aggressive intravenous chemotherapy before they could check whether the cancer was in remission.

The entire treatment would take place over a period of nearly eighteen months.

CHAPTER SIX

GREAT FAITH

When Dr. Taylor discussed my course of treatment, I felt fear began to threaten my shield of faith.

You thought your cancer was at either stage zero or stage one. You have believed with all your might that you would not need all that treatment. Then suddenly, you are told that you are one step away from where there is nothing they can do for you medically.

Furthermore, y o u need every medical a r s e n a l t o a g g r e s s i v e l y attack that cancer. Is not that extremely challenging to your faith?

The treatment journey became a constant battle in my mind – to walk in blind faith or look at the circumstances and open up to fear. I knew I had a hard road ahead.

You have all the faith for stage zero or stage one, but one step to terminal cancer? It was like a big punch in the gut. What are you going to do now?

It looked like my faith walk was upgraded to the Accelerated School of Faith. It was one thing to have faith for myself and lay hold of the LORD's assurances concerning the road ahead. But what about those who I would leave behind? Their faith was enough to believe a healing for a stage zero or stage one colorectal cancer only. What would they do?

I went home and passed on the information to my family and close friends. Everyone who had been standing with me in faith for stage zero or stage one cancer was distraught. Sadness and despair had descended upon my home once again.

And that is where I needed great faith.

Like most adolescents, I had experienced some rough patches growing up with my mother. When she came for those two weeks, she cried many tears. Whenever I would be upstairs, she will be downstairs talking to Terrence. She would say, "Why not me? I used to beat her a lot when she was growing up. Why can't I have this cancer? Why does it have to be my child?" Those were heart-wrenching moments. What can one say? It was the love of a mother crying for a child she may have to bury before her time. It was extremely difficult for everyone. Their faith within the circumstance could carry them only so far.

My children were broken. They cried often. I found myself wondering how they would survive the next few months of treatments I had to endure. My family had prepared for the worst case scenario – death. Yet it was at that point that the LORD moved me to the School of Great Faith.

It is one thing to have faith for yourself but it is quite different to have faith for yourself and the other people who, not only do not have faith, but also are unable to even try to have one. When people around you are focused on circumstances and they are determined to even prepare for the worst case scenario, you have to carry them with you. You have to have faith for yourself and for them – that is great faith.

When the Roman Centurion sought the LORD Jesus Christ for the healing of his servant, Jesus was willing to go with him. However, the centurion who understood authority said to the LORD, "I am a man under authority. When I command this soldier to do a task, he will do it. I am not worthy for you to come all the way to my house to heal my servant. Simply send a word and he will be healed."

The centurion had left a household that was prepared for the death of that sick servant. He had to have faith for himself, for that sick servant, and for the entire household. He has to have that great amount of faith to believe that healing would happen once he encountered the LORD. He had faith that a mere word from the LORD, even at a distant place, was enough to send healing.

Jesus Christ marveled at him and said, "I have never seen such great faith in all of Israel." He declared the healing of centurion's servant and it was later reported that in that same hour, the servant was healed (Luke 7:2-10).

I had to practice that level of great faith – believing for the sake of others. I would ask my family, "What are you crying for? Don't you see that the LORD will heal me? I am being set up for great miracles."

I was changing the atmosphere. The LORD was building in me the character of faith. I believe that the LORD was preparing me to minister to people with faith-defying circumstances. I had to experience it in order to most effectively minister to them.

This meant that I had to build a bulwark of faith – from little to great faith. Character is not built in isolation. Not even Jesus could build character in isolation. It is built by interacting with people and responding to the things that happen to and through you.

There were times when I felt low, yet, I had to hold other people's hands. I would go to the closet, break down and cry. The LORD is the only One Who is stronger than me. When

Diagnosis: Cancer

I think of that season, I can say with the psalmist in Psalm 116:1-9:

```
I love the LORD, for He heard my voice,
        He heard my cry for mercy.
    Because He turned His ear to me,
  I will call on Him as long as I live.
    The cords of death entangled me,
The anguish of the grave came over me;
I was overcome by distress and sorrow.
Then I called on the name of the LORD:
"LORD, save me!"
  The LORD is gracious and righteous;
      Our God is full of compassion.
    The LORD protects the unwary;
When I was brought low, He saved me.
    Return to your rest, my soul, For
      the LORD has been good to you.
For You, LORD, have delivered me from
              death,
        My eyes from tears,
      My feet from stumbling,
    That I may walk before the LORD
    In the land of the living.
```

Into His strong arms, I would collapse and unravel my feelings. Then, the Holy Spirit would encourage me and I would wipe my tears, go out, and be strong again. I had to be strong for everyone. Their faith depended on my strength. I was their faith gauge. If I crumbled, they would crumble with me. If I was strong, then they would draw on that strength. It was not easy at all but those moments built in me a strong faith in the LORD and really prepared me for the treatment journey ahead.

The Journey

Once the flex sig was done and the entire treatment regimen prescribed, I handed it all to the LORD. I told Him to let only His will be done in my life even with the intervention of medical technology. I prayed for the medical personnel who would work on me. I did not want another experience of fear through a medical staff.

I had three weeks of various tests and blood work before I began radiation and chemotherapy.

In one of the Sundays, during service, my pastor called and prophesied unto me that I was embarking on a journey I had to take. That same night, Ericka called me from Fort Myers. She told me that she had a dream about me and shared it with her pastor. He interpreted that I was going on a journey and she would be beside me. It was a confirmation of what the LORD was showing me. My faith was strengthened further.

Three months before I wrote this book, I had a dream. I Was with Abraham of the Bible. He put me on a horse and said, "You are going on a journey." He said to stay on the horse and don't get off. My journey continues to date.

Total Surrender

During those three weeks of medical tests and preparation for the radiation and chemotherapy, I resolved to spend quality time with my family. I wanted to operate contrary to what my health was saying. I was going to enjoy every moment. This is a journal entry from June 3, 2010:

God is so good, I woke up to see another day. I'm alive and healthy. I have clothes, food, shelter and a loving family. We had family prayer and Ladarris really shocked me today. His prayer was awesome. God, I am enjoying what you are doing in my family.

I took Zari to Chuck E. Cheese today. I really enjoyed my time with my granddaughter. I know that she is gifted, talented and anointed.

This is my season of sowing. I know my reaping time is coming. I am sitting here listening to "Inspiration Today" and it is talking about sowing a seed. I know that God is telling me to sow like never before.

I know that obedience is better than sacrifice. Jesus is LORD. God, bless us indeed. Enlarge our territory. Keep your hands on us to keep us from evil so that we will not cause harm in Jesus' Name, Amen!

During those three weeks, I was inspired to rehearse a prophetic dance of submission to the song *Yes* by *Shekinah Glory*. That song had really ministered to me.

So, I practiced the dance presentation and on that Sunday before I began my treatment, I presented it before the congregation. Terrence and his stepmother, Janette, who was in town for a family reunion attended church with me that day. The gist of the song is as follows:

```
Will your heart and soul say, yes?
Will your Spirit still say, yes?
There is more that I require of thee.
If I told you what I really need.
Will your heart and soul say, yes?

I'll say, Yes, Yes! My soul says yes.
My mind says, my heart says yes, yes.
    Yes, I will Jesus, Yes, Yes!

  I'll do what you want me to do.
  I'll say what you want me to say.
  I'll go, if you lead me,

      I won't be afraid.
    I'll step out on Your Word.
        My soul says
      Yes, yes, yes, yes!
```

No one had ever seen me dance before so they were astonished and was blessed by the dance. Through that dance, I yielded myself to the LORD releasing my own will and taking His will. I wanted the LORD to know that I love Him and was saying, *yes, yes, yes* to His will and His way.

Throughout my treatment regimen, total surrender became my theme. I continually had to ask the LORD to have His way in each event; whether I understood or not, whether I liked what was happening or not.

45

Diagnosis: Cancer

Whenever I read through my journal entries, I realize that since I made that initial decision to surrender every step to the LORD, it seemed to have become part of my lifestyle and thought pattern. I noticed many entries where I wrote, "Have your way, LORD."

The next day, a Monday, I started the five week radiation and chemotherapy treatment.

CHAPTER SEVEN

THE TREATMENT JOURNEY

School was out and I decided that our children should go down to Florida for summer. I did not know what to expect from the treatment and I did not know how ill I would get. Actually, I expected the worst possible reaction to the daily radiation and chemotherapy. I imagined body hair loss, nausea, weakness, among other things. Worse, I imagined my inability to even function at all. You think of chemotherapy and you think of those that I mentioned.

I would shake all of those imaginations away for I did not want my children to see me go through that ordeal. I needed them to remain strong and hopeful.

So, Terrence took them to Florida and I was basically home alone. It was the second day of my treatment when they left. I was very well. By leaving me home alone, it gave them the feeling that I was all right with everything.

One of the sisters from church was to stay with me, but she was afraid to drive on the highway. I did not mind. I stayed in the house all by myself.

That first week, I drove myself back and forth from the medical center. Surprisingly, the first week of chemotherapy and radiation was not that bad. Everything was fine during those first few rounds of treatment. I was thinking: *This is not bad at all.* At worst, I would come home a little light-headed after the treatments. The first week was not bad, but it was just a teaser. Soon, I started having the radiation therapy in my abdomen and rectum. The treatment is getting painful. I remember writing in my journal:

The enemy is turning up the heat!

That first week, I would go to church every day after the chemo a n d radiation t r e a t m e n t. Everything seemed fine. I thought I could handle it. But soon after, I began to get much weaker and lonelier more than ever. I remember writing about it often. My journal entry for June 18, 2010 reads:

The revival at church was good and was very much needed. Terrence's family reunion last weekend was nice. His father and stepmom came and stayed at our house.

His dad told a few of the family members about my diagnosis. At first, I was a little shocked because I didn't want anyone to know, but, I know that he was just really concerned.

I danced at church on Sunday to Shekinah Glory's "Yes." I give God all the glory because my body was saying No, but my spirit has a Yes.

Every since the kids left, I felt as if I am all alone. I know that I have God but I expected that Terrence would be home all the time to be with me, but, everyone is moving like everything is normal.

Does anyone not know what I am feeling? I know that I have to hold on. It has taken such a toll on me, even spiritually. I haven't been studying like I was. I just lie down all day and night. LORD, help me! I just want for Your will to be done.

The Treatment Journey

During those days, my godmother, Evangelist *Adrienne Hayes "Mama A" (3/23/1955 to 10/29/2012)*, came and stayed all week with me.

On my second week of treatment, I managed to continue going to church after chemo and radiation. However, I would come back home with a fever each day. It was because the treatment were light-sensitive. Any exposure to the sun or light in general was to be avoided.

I had been advised that if I got a fever any time after the Treatment, I should immediately go to hospital. I was so scared of hospitals and felt I would only go if I absolutely had to. So, I would take aspirin or Tylenol tablets, attend the church Bible study, and generally keep myself in prayer. However, every time I went to the church Bible study, I would be down with fever because of the long hours of light exposure.

Whenever I reflect on that period, I knew that at the back of my mind, I believed that I was not effectively exercising my faith for miraculous divine healing if I go to the hospital for the fever. I did not realize that modern medicine was just one of the many methods which the LORD was using in my faith journey to health (see Appendix II).

In my pursuit for divine healing, Mama A was a voice of wisdom. I had been feverish and self-medicating when she said to me, "Alicia you've got to go to the hospital. Your fever is fluctuating seriously. You cannot take a chance." It was wise advice so I took it.

We called the nurse and were advised to get to the hospital immediately. I was made to receive the much dreaded blood transfusion. Immediately, my body reacted to the blood transfusion and more medication was pumped into me. After I had stabilized, I went back home.

Diagnosis: Cancer

My days outside the hospital were spent in prayer. Every opportunity I had, I went to the church. But with each visit to the church, I had to go back to hospital. The doctor told me, "You will not be able to go to church anymore. Your immune system is weakening because you are undergoing chemo and radiation." Generally, exposure to the elements was not helping me. But I told him, "No, I have to go to church. That is where my help comes from."

He then asked me, "Can't you watch church on the television or internet?" But I was unyielding, so I kept going. And each time I went to church, I would get so ill and be forced to get back to the hospital. Finally, I had to be admitted for a week because the fever would not go down and my hip started to swell. They could not tell what was wrong with me for I was under so much medication.

During that week in hospital, I finally realized that I could take church with me wherever I went.

The entire time I was in the hospital, I had a little audio-player. I would listen to prophetic praise and worship all day and all night. I would read my Bible and encourage myself in the LORD. My journal entry for July 24, 2010 reads:

I was so happy to get out of the hospital after 5 days. I am just happy to be home and for some reason, I am dreaming a lot. I guess that is just the LORD's way of telling me to pray for these individuals.

My treatment journey was long and tedious in many ways and I must share about my destiny helpers as they were

The Treatment Journey

Major faith boosters in this travel. They came alongside this journey and kept me encouraged all the way.

Diagnosis: Cancer

CHAPTER EIGHT

DESTINY HELPERS

Destiny helpers are people whom the LORD will bring to your way to help you fulfill a redemptive purpose. They will be part of your life when you are walking in obedience to the LORD's will.

The LORD would not, in any circumstance, send helpers to your path when you are walking on your own or the enemy's rebellious way; totally contrary to His purposes in your life. He will not help you plunge into your own destruction.

Destiny helpers may be people whom you might have known for a long time. Sometimes, they are the people whom you encountered for a short span of time; for a certain period. And once the season is over, you might never have the chance to meet them again. Others may be not-so-pleasant. However, their impact in your life is positive and unforgettable.

Right from the beginning of my faith journey, the LORD had prepared a whole host of destiny helpers like the wonderful medical team that took part in my entire treatment journey. There were also many others whom I may not have mentioned in this book, but to each of those precious people, the LORD has placed you in His book of remembrance.

When I began the treatment regimen, I noticed that the hand of the LORD was truly upon me. God literally gave me angelic human agents for my medical care. Right from the cancer specialist, to   the nurses, and to the other medical aides I

Encountered throughout the journey, I met people whom I would put in the same league as angels.

My nurse practitioner, Miss Angela, was from Africa. She was an angel. My insurance would not cover my chemotherapy medication that cost close to two thousand US dollars.

Miss Angela learned about my plight and said that she would figure out a way to help me with my financial situation. She would come every time to check how I was doing. She would tell me she was thinking about me. She released such positive energy in every word she said and everything she did.

Miss Mary was my Clinical Trial nurse. She was caring and informative. She made me understand the process. She was very pleasant and I considered her my angel, too.

Because medical treatment was the prescription I believe the LORD had for me, He had strategically placed God-fearing, pleasant nurses and doctors to work with me. Even in the waiting area, I encountered pleasant fellow patients whose stories encouraged and increased my faith. I too, found people to encourage at every visit. It seemed to me that the LORD had arranged for everything.

I do not even remember when the LORD sorted out the challenge with regard to the insurance payments for my chemotherapy, but the insurance company decided to cover my entire treatment. It could only be the LORD's doing.

My Godmother, "Mama A" to whose memory I dedicate this book, was my major tower of strength. She surely was one of my greatest destiny helpers. She stayed within my reach all throughout this journey. She went back and forth on a three-hour flight just so she could be with me all the time. Of all the people who came to stay, she spent the most time with me.

I remember making some entries in my journal which read as follows:

July 17, 2010

It seems like it's been a while since I've written in my journal. God has got to have something in store for me. I was bored and Terrence was going to Unity Day. It's an event in Alabama where everyone goes to the park. I refused to remain in the house and felt that I needed to get out, too.

So, I went to the park. After getting there, I totally regretted it. Later, when I went to sleep that night, I had a dream showing that the bottom of my feet turned black. I knew the LORD was telling me that I had walked on unholy grounds. He was saying that this was a time for me to be in the perfect will of God.

I just had to get out of the house for it seems like everyone is going on about their business. Ladarris doesn't call, the kids are enjoying themselves in Florida and Terrence is acting like everything is normal. Everyone have their own agendas. I just feel so alone. I can't wait until Mama A arrives. I will have her here to keep me company.

July 19, 2010

Mama A arrived and we went to eat. Afterwards, I started feeling sick. I ended up getting admitted to the hospital again. For the most time, I was there by myself. I felt all alone. I really didn't tell anyone that I was in the hospital again because I just didn't want anyone to know my business. I don't want to deal with the negativity.

Diagnosis: Cancer

I don't know what I would have done without her during those times. She went to doctor's appointments with me. She was strong in faith and full of wise counsel. She helped me understand that my medical treatment could be a prescription from the LORD.

When she went to be with the LORD on October 29, 2012, her best friend told me, "Your momma loved you. When you were sick, she was so concerned about you. When you were going back and forth to hospital, she would say to me, 'I hope I don't lose my daughter.'"

My other destiny helpers include my beloved husband, Terrence, was a tower of strength in the background, my children and my mother, my Pastor and First Lady, Bishop and Prophetess Franklin, Grandma Dorothy Smith, Brenda Young, and Sharon Adams, Nakia Toney.

Another destiny helper was Prophetess Franklin. She communicated with me on a daily basis. I even requested my pastor at that time, Pastor James Griffin, to allow her to come and carry out a three-day revival at our church. It was she who later came with a team that includes Sister Ebony, Tiki and Mother Jones and spent four days with me. They were true powerful women of prayer and destiny helpers in my time of need.

The company of spiritual leaders, numerous prayer partners who prayed through the season is just too many to mention. They, too, helped to pass the baton of destiny as I walked this faith journey.

Sometimes, your experience with some people may not be very pleasant. That is not uncommon. However, it all depends on how you handle those unpleasant experiences. If you consider even bad people as your destiny helpers and choose to develop a positive outlook from the encounters you had with them, then, the outcome would be helpful for you.

For instance, Judas Iscariot's impact on the life of Jesus Christ was very negative. He betrayed the LORD and set Him up for His death. Yet, the impact of that betrayal was salvation for all of creation because Jesus chose to turn that negative betrayal into a positive salvation.

When a person uses the perfumes and cosmetics manufactured by Estee Lauder, they know that they are using one of the finest cosmetics products in the world of beauty and high fashion. Even those who aren't experts in the field of cosmetics and fragrances recognize this prominent and respected name. Estee Lauder, the company that was started by a fiercely ambitious ninth child of a Jewish immigrant family in Corona, Queens, New York, is now a household name.

Estee Lauder, born Josephine Ester Mentzer, is a somewhat mysterious figure for little is known of her formative years. She lived in a room situated above her father's hardware store. She started her enterprise by selling skin creams concocted by her uncle, a chemist, in beauty shops, beach clubs and resorts.

It is said that at one time while working as a sales girl promoting her beauty products in one shop, a lady of high-class came into the shop to purchase some products.

As she passed by Estee, the fascinating scent of lady's perfume enthralled her. Estee approached the lady and complimented her by saying that she found her perfume absolutely wonderful. The lady was very thankful so Estee proceeded to ask for the name of the perfume. The lady told her. Estee said that when she gets a hold of money enough to buy the perfume, she would make sure she gets that scent for herself, too.

Diagnosis: Cancer

On hearing that, the lady turned to her with utter contempt. She looked at Estee from head to foot and told her, "How can low-class people like you dare to desire the same type of perfume that someone like me wears?" From that moment on, Estee resolved that she would design the kind of perfume and cosmetics that this "type of woman" would scuttle to purchase.

A seemingly bad encounter with an unsuspecting destiny helper pushed Estee to become one of the most famous and successful geniuses of modern day cosmetics and fragrances industry.

*Today, **Estee Lauder** has become the largest privately owned Cosmetics Company in the world with sales well in excess of one billion dollars* (www.esteelauder.com).

You don't automatically get to have only nice people as your destiny helpers. God can use even the unpleasant ones if you will surrender them all to Him. When you think about it, the awful relationships that you want to do away with most of the time, are the ones that sharpen you. When iron sharpens iron, it is not a pleasant feeling.

In my case, I had to close down the businesses I had started and stay at home to focus on my treatment. I even had to relocate from Alabama back to Tampa Florida later on. It seemed that everything I had worked on gradually turned to ashes.

There were those who spoke such negativity about my situation. Some said I was dying and others went to the extent of saying that I had died. It was as if they did not wish me well at all. Some would call and say such hard and insensitive things about my condition. It was as if they were rejoicing over my ill-fortune.

Destiny Helpers

Surprisingly, those words did not shake or offend me much. They gave me the fortitude to continue the fight in my faith journey. Not only did I become more determined to get well, but I also wanted to look good while I was at it. I made up my mind. One day, I would go back into business and become successful at it again.

These unpleasant people were destiny helpers because of their negativity. Their destructive words were like stones that were being hurled at me. I chose to turn those destructive stones into stepping-stones to get to my next level with the LORD.
Never react negatively to haters. Always let their stones of destructive words and actions that are hurled at you become your stepping-stones into your destiny. One day, you will thank them for it.

Diagnosis: Cancer

CHAPTER NINE

CONTROLLING THE ATMOSPHERE

In my journal entry for June 25, 2010, I wrote:

I woke up so sick this morning. The enemy is putting me down. My husband is back. He woke up and had to pick up his car. I am heading to the doctor to get my medication. I have just been listening to Juanita Bynum's "Soul Cry".

Whatcha' gonna do
When you don't know who to turn to
And whatcha' gonna say
When you don't know what to pray

And where you're gonna run
When you don't know where to hide
And whatcha' gonna do
When the pain just won't subside

At times when I feel like I am all alone, I know I have God. However, I feel I have no family support in Alabama like what I would have in Florida.

I had been undergoing daily treatment for about four weeks. I had people around me and was not alone, but I feel I was walking a lonely journey. My husband was there but I often felt removed, lonely. I sometimes thought that maybe because his mother had suddenly died years prior to my condition, it was especially difficult for him.

By that time, I had closed down my business and never left the house except to go to the doctor's office. I was not going to church much either, but I would pray all day.

Terrence would tell me, "I have to get out of the house." I felt like he did not want to stay with me, but then, I guess he had to deal with that season in his own way. We were walking together, but each of us was so desperately lonely.

By the time people found out that I was unwell, I was coming to the end of my treatment. Even then, some of the phone calls I got were simply mean. Some people would say "I hear you're dying."

I was getting so much negativity over phone calls and rumors in the city. "She closed down her business because she has cancer." One time, a rumor had spread saying that I had died. Others said I was relocating back home to Florida because I was about to die.

If you are not strong in the LORD and you allow such words to go unchallenged, you can go down. Because of those ill-spoken words, I had to control the atmosphere. I would continually counter them with Biblical truths and proclaim, "I am healed."

It was tiresome sometimes, but it was like continually deodorizing my atmosphere with words of life, health and peace. I guarded my spiritual space zealously because I did not want to hear the negativity. It was a deliberate choice on my part, and the consequence was nobody would call and check on me. It compounded to my loneliness.

Controlling The Atmosphere

Some of my ex-employees, people who I thought were friends, kept saying that I was dying. It is difficult when the people you expect would speak life into the situation, turn around, and speak negativity toward you. You feel like they want you to die.

It got to a point where I came to thinking, who is for me? Who is against me? I felt like nobody but the LORD was on my side. I had to continually encourage myself in Him.

The enemy's onslaught against my shield of faith was relentless and it was building up to a head. My journal entries on June 22 and June 23, 2010 read as follows:

June 22, 2010
Terrence left to go to Florida, so, Sis. Brenda and Janet came and stayed over as I went to my treatment. We went to Olive Garden and fellowshipped and came home. Brenda and Janice left the next day and I was home alone again. I just drove myself to the doctor. That's when the spirit of loneliness really crept in.

June 23, 2010
I went to my treatment. I was going to just stay home and cry out to the LORD, but God told me to go to the revival. The revival was awesome. Prophet Butler told me that He saw angels all around me leaping and saying HEALED! God is so good. He also prayed for me. God has so much in store for me and the enemy is just mad. My heart, soul and mind say Yes!

Diagnosis: Cancer

One moment, the enemy would try to knock me down with discouragement and the next, the LORD would lift me up again through a song, a sermon and, most of all, a prophet.

Around that time, I was admitted into the hospital again. It was in those times in the hospital when I felt the loneliest. Looking back over that period, I realized that the loneliness was a result of seeing everyone around me busy with their activities.

I am not an idle person. In fact, I am very sociable and I like to work hard. It was not easy to sit back and watch everyone else put their energies to work while I literally lie down. Whenever somebody comes to visit me, I noticed that they just came to see me for thirty minutes or an hour and then leave after that because they have other agendas.

A lot of times while lying down in my hospital bed, I would face the window and cry to God asking, *Why me? Why am I going through this? I feel so all alone.*

I began to wonder if anybody really cared. In that dark place, I would think: *Everyone is having the time of their lives. It is summer.* My husband, at that time, was trying to get his antique car restored. I felt the car was more important to him than me.

My sister, kids and friends were not calling. And so, in that place of such dark thoughts, my whole view of the world was distorted. I interpreted everything through depressive, negative perceptions. I felt such a deep cloud of loneliness. Depression threatened me.

Finally, I was released from the hospital. When we got home, my husband had to go to Eufaula which is twenty-five minutes away from our home in Fort Mitchell. I told him I did not want to be in the house by myself. But he had to go, and therefore left. It was at that point that the cloud of depression apparently opened up and descended hard. Everything I had held on to – the faith, the strength – literally left as Terrence went out.

I went to my daughter's room and phoned her. They were still in Florida for summer. I started the conversation like this: "Whatever happens to me, whatever else you do, I want you to promise me that you will graduate. I want you to make me proud."

She said, "Mama, what's wrong?" I started crying. I just told her "I am tired." She said to me, "Mama, please don't say that." I said, "I am tired. I want to go home and be with the LORD. I want you to make me some promises. I am alone and I am just so tired."

Jasmine asked me, "Where is Papa?" I insisted, "He is not here. It does not matter. Just make me some promises." That had to be the lowest point in my journey.

By the time I finished speaking to Jasmine, there was another call waiting, so we hung up and I picked up the next call. It was my sister, Ericka.

The first thing she asked was, "What is wrong with you?" I said, "I am so tired. I am ready to go. I cannot take it anymore. I am ready to go and be with the LORD." At that point I had been crying too much.

Ericka told me with a voice of such authority and power, "Who are you? Who do you think you are? God is not finished with you. How dare you say you are tired? It is not up to you. It is not your choice. You shall live, you shall not die."

The moment she said that, it was as if something in me was ignited by fire. I got off the bed of affliction and began to decree and declare that I was healed.

Diagnosis: Cancer

I began to war in the spirit – against the spirit of death in the house, depression, oppression and every wicked spirit that had been fighting against my faith. I began to speak life and buoyancy. I reminded the LORD of His promise I could recall concerning my life and future.

Death had come knocking and I was about to succumb to that spirit. That was what made me realize that many people die prematurely because they roll over, give up, and do not fight back.

I remembered right there that sickness, death, and financial shortages are all spirits under the control of the devil. The Bible tells us to resist the devil and he will flee (James 4:7). I only needed to arise and say NO! That is the first step, and then I continued to say NO to him and whatever he was throwing at me.

Even when I had faltered and wanted to give in right there, the LORD had put another destiny helper in my way. At that moment when I was falling, there was someone, my own sister, to catch me and lift me up again. I will never forget that moment; and I bless the LORD for her life-saving call.

If it were not for Ericka, I would have given up. The fight in me was out. The enemy used my loneliness to bring depression. And hot on the heels of depression, death was knocking.

In those few moments from when Terrence left and my conversation with Jasmine, I was ready to give up. God knew what I needed and literally rebuked that spirit right out of me through Ericka's powerful life-giving words of faith. I was immediately infected by faith.

Truly, the power of life and death are on the tip of our tongues (Proverbs 18:21). I merely had to speak a negative word, and the effect was immediate – I wanted to die. I was going down. In the twinkling of an eye, death can come to me. He is very sneaky. Yet within those very moments, when I picked up my sister's call and said those words of death, she spoke life and immediately, I felt as though virtue came out of her and into me.

I was ready to live again. I felt I could face anything. I got empowered and virtually resurrected. Since that moment, I never had a day of depression or yearning for death again. Ericka, my vital destiny helper!

Sanitizing the Atmosphere

Whenever you release negativity through your words or emotions, or even when you allow yourself to listen or watch or read negative stuff, it is like toxic soot blown into your atmosphere. It will literally saturate everything around you.

After my sister spoke into my life and the depression lifted off, I prayed. I felt that I was back on track and energized to continue with the treatment. However, I did not realize that although I was delivered from the spirit of death, it was still lurking about waiting for an opportunity when I would crumble again, or when someone would say something mean or do something negative. Death found an entrance in my life.

Again, the LORD sent destiny helpers to come to sanitize my atmosphere.

My old pastor, Prophetess Franklin and a couple of mighty women of God came too. Pastor Griffin allowed Prophetess Franklin to minister in a three-day revival in Eufaula, Alabama. These ladies spent some days with me. They said, "There is a spirit of death real bad in this house." I was surprised. I told them what had happened with my moment of depression. My journal entry for July 26, 2010 reads:

Prophetess Franklin, Pastor Jones, Evangelist Ebony and Sister Tiki; all of them just blessed my soul. They came for the revival and stayed an extra day with me and it was nice. God knew just what I needed because before they came, there was a bad spirit of oppression and depression that had come on me till

Controlling The Atmosphere

I was begging God to take me home (like He really was, just because I said so. What a Joke!).

The conference at church was awesome. God showed up and showed out. Terence left Saturday to go pick up the kids so when Prophetess and everyone left, I was home alone again. I've just been resting. Kia came and took me to my appointment today and cleaned up for me. I thank God for her being here for me today.

The spirit of death did not only affect me, but it touched everything. It seemed like everything had died. My daily routine did not go beyond my going to hospital and staying in the house. My businesses had died. And it seemed that my marriage would die too.

Those ladies travailed and warred with the spirit of death and broke its power over my life and endeavors. They ushered in healing and life over my household. By the time they left, there was a new release in every area of our lives.

Throughout the journey, I had a lot of mighty men and women of God praying and helping me command my atmosphere. In controlling the atmosphere, the biggest defilers are negative words and emotions. Negative emotions are fuel for the enemy. Do not give him the privilege to wrestle you down.

No matter what anyone says, remember that the power of life and death is in the tongue. There will always be faith wreckers, the naysayers. When they speak negatively, immediately chop it down with your own words of life and truth from the Word of God. You need to read and hear the Word of God in every available format. There are countless scriptures on healing which you can speak into your life.

Diagnosis: Cancer

Sometimes you may not have the opportunity to cancel what someone is saying immediately. However, do not take it lying down. When you have a moment, cancel those words and speak life over yourself and your circumstance. Do not give negativity a chance to take root. Cut it down immediately. Ask the LORD to bring destiny helpers who will pick you up when you are weary.

The Bible says that the LORD is our very Present Help in times of trouble (Psalm 46:1). Remember, He uses people – destiny helpers. Ask that He will align them with the journey you are taking so that when you get to that difficult spot; there will be divine help for you in that time of need. It is you who switches on your television and choose what you want to watch. Is it helping your situation?

It is you who turns the dial on the radio and choose what You want to hear. Is it life-giving and encouraging? It is you who can pick up a life-giving encouraging book to read. Nobody will do it for you.

It is you who choose the kind of people you will allow yourself to be around in your difficult circumstance. Do they enable life or bring death?

The kind of atmosphere you will have will enable or disable healing. It will enable or disable success in every aspect of your life. Granted, there is a price to pay when you choose the way of the LORD. You may get lonely, but it is only for a season. You may miss out on a few activities, but He will provide you with other better opportunities at the right time.

You may feel you are losing, but in Him, you gain life abundant. Choosing the LORD in your space, rather than everything else, is the best choice you can make. Even when you fall, He will catch you, like He did for me so many times.

Controlling The Atmosphere

Nobody will control your atmosphere for you; you must take responsibility for it and never get weary of speaking life and blessing over yourself, and remind the LORD of the promises in His word concerning your life. I have made some of these promises available in the daily journal that goes with this book.

Start from there and change your atmosphere. This works for your marriage, your employment, your relationships, and every part of your life. Take charge, sanitize and then take control of your atmosphere.

Diagnosis: Cancer

CHAPTER TEN

PROPHETIC PROMISES

My journal entry for June 19, 2010 reads as follows:

I had a dream that I went to Prophetess Bynum's church and she gave me the date, July 20, and stated that she would come to Mt. Olive and do a revival free of charge because I had favor with God.

In the dream, as I went inside her church, they sat me in the front row. Wow! I don't know what that dream meant and the date July 20. Have your way LORD.

Then eight days later, on June 27, this is what I wrote:

Today is the day the LORD has made. I woke up with expectancy this morning. I and Terrence went to Atlanta to Prophetess Bynum's church. We got there late and as I was trying to rush because we were late. I heard a small still voice say, "The last shall be first, and the first shall be last."

As we got closer to the door, I could feel the anointing. The worship was amazing. As we walked in, we filled out a visitor form. And as we were about to sit down, the usher came and took us to the very front row. I immediately remembered the dream I had days prior, that I was going to sit on the front row.

It was a sad day at her church because one of her spiritual daughters died in a car accident. Prophetess Bynum gave an awesome message and there was one time that she looked me in the eyes and said, "We will live and not die." I just felt she was speaking directly at me.

I really enjoyed the service and the LORD told me that I would be going back again. I can't wait! Have your way LORD!

Oh, I almost forgot! Prophet Butler had his administrator call and check on me as well. I told her that his prophecies are coming to pass. He had prophesied that my dreams would be coming to pass.

I thought that was very special for him to call and check on me since he found out about my temporary illness. God is allowing me to connect with some powerful men and women of God. I just thank God for all my trials, tribulations and betrayals, etc.

I have received numerous prophetic promises in many forms in my walk with the LORD. Prophetic promises are words from the LORD which are given at specific seasons in your life. These promises come especially in times when you are about to embark on a tough journey ahead or when you are in a difficult situation, and the LORD wants to encourage you.

From the time I began to sense that something was seriously wrong with my health, I felt like it was as if the LORD had increased the number of prophetic promises I had received. Those were such powerful words that encouraged me, but they also made me a little anxious for what was coming ahead.

When I was still young in my Christianity, I was like a child waiting expectantly for Father Christmas to come and bring his goodies each time I receive a prophetic promise. I did not realize that prophetic promises come in the context of battle or distress.

For instance, when the LORD promised me that He would open up a certain door meant to establish a new business venture; I was excited and confident that the door would surely open. I did not expect that He was giving that promise because the circumstances surrounding that door would threaten to shut me out. When the trials had come, I would become so discouraged and angry with God. *Why did He say He would open that door and yet there are so many hindrances?* I expected that if the LORD spoke a promise, it would be smooth-sailing all the way to its fulfillment. Through time, I learned that when a promise came from the LORD, it was in the context of a great battle ahead. Therefore, I can't help but to feel the twinge of anxiety that comes with each promise.

In the Bible, whenever the LORD send any one of His servants on a challenging journey, He would always give them great and spectacular promises. When the LORD asked Abram to travel away from his country, his people and his father's household into the unknown Promised Land, He had to back that challenge with a promise. He said to Abram, *"Go from your country, your people and your father's household to the land I will show you. I will make you into a great nation, and I will bless you; I will make your name great, and you will be a blessing. I will bless those who bless you, and whoever curses you I will curse; and all peoples on earth will be blessed through you"* (Genesis 12:1-3).

Diagnosis: Cancer

That was a great prophetic promise. As you read the story of Abram, you can see the great trials he underwent, yet the promises were there to undergird him in each season.

When you read the book of Exodus, you see the great promises the LORD had made to Moses. He promised to be with Moses and do exploits through him (Exodus 3:12, 14-22, 4:16). The LORD even told Moses, *"I will make you as God before pharaoh and Aaron will be your prophet"* (Exodus 7:1). He was promising Moses His own Presence and Authority as He did wonders that brought down the existing superpower of his day – ancient Egypt. When you see the exceedingly great challenges that Moses had to face, then you begin to understand the great prophetic promises that were needed to undergird him as he walked that difficult road as Israel's deliverer.

Again, when you read the book of Joshua, it opens with some of the most popular and well-loved prophetic promises of all time. The LORD encouraged Joshua to be strong and courageous. He was assured that everywhere he put the soles of his feet would be his territory (Joshua 1:1-9). Joshua had the task of defeating thirty-one kings on that side of Jordan in order to take over the Promised Land. Then, he would subdivide it among the twelve tribes of Israel. He was the first warrior to serve as leader of God's chosen people, and he needed strong prophetic promises to lean on as he warred and overthrew kingdom after kingdom.

When Jesus Christ commissioned the apostles to teach all nations, He, too, gave them prophetic promises to undergird the Great Commission (Matthew 28:18-20; Mark16:15-18). He promised that he would be with them always, and that they would receive the Holy Spirit to help them in the task ahead (Acts 1:4). He promised them blessings from His Father both in this world and in the world to come. They had the daunting task of laying the foundations of what has to become the greatest and most formidable movement on earth for all time – the Body of Christ. They were doing it in an environment that was completely contrary to the patterns of God's kingdom. However, the prophetic promises have been there to undergird every generation of the Church of Christ.

Learn that whenever you receive a prophetic promise, you are about to embark on a difficult journey ahead and it will require active faith and increased prayer. You need to obediently hear the LORD and constantly guard yourself against any counter-attack you may get against that promise. If the LORD says doors will open for you, expect that you will encounter forces that will try to close those doors. Those are counter- attacks of the devil against your prophetic promise.

I had journals full of written prophecies over my life. And it was during those difficult days of walking through the treatment that I would re-read my old journals and pull out every prophetic word that was said to me to remind the LORD of His promise and to encourage myself about what the LORD had said before.

A wise man had said, **"Never doubt after the storm, What the LORD said before the storm."** Those prophetic promises were the anchor that I needed during those storms in my life. I have recorded a few of the ones that specifically declared the faith journey I was on. The Bible says in Psalm 119:140, *"Your promises have been thoroughly tested; that is why I love them so much."*

Everything that had occurred over the month of May 2010 was both overwhelming and heartbreaking. All I could think of was the prophetic promises that I had received in months prior to my illness.

Diagnosis: Cancer

Preceding the diagnosis, there were a lot of revivals in the city and we were going to all of them. I remember my friend Brenda calling to tell me that there was a revival service at Browns Memorial Church and there was a mighty man of God, Prophet Jolando Butler, coming to minister.

Deep inside, I knew that I would be facing a mighty Battle. So, we went to the revival and Prophet Butler preached on The *Paradigm Shift*. After he preached his sermon and was about to leave the pulpit to go back to his seat, he turned around and came down to us, pointed at me and prophesied over my life.

It struck me when he said that, "An angel has his foot on your rooftop saying Victory!" He also said that God favored me.

I then knew that if an angel was saying, "Victory!" over my rooftop, then there was a battle coming. However, I felt relieved in hearing the prophet say that God favored me. I knew I would be all right. Prophet Butler also told me that the LORD had said that I would sit among kings and queens. Those were some of the words that the prophet proclaimed over my life that night. My journal entry on May 28, 2010 reads:

LORD, I know that you have given me the ability to endure all the trials and tribulations. I know I can endure all of it and come out as pure gold. On May 24, 2010, the doctors informed me that my biopsy showed that my tumor was cancerous and the diagnosis was colorectal cancer.

My first response was why? For the past three weeks I Had been receiving prophecies, calling and anointing regarding my life, but never about my health. I know that God does not want me to focus on the problem but on the promises.

I know that the road ahead will be rough but I know that God will be with me all the way. He loves me so much that He sent an angel for me during my colonoscopy. My mom and Ericka were worrying about me but God sent them a message through a dream. As I look over my life, I can just see God's hand on my life since I was young.

There are times that I do wonder how long this will take and what toll on my family this will bring. But I believe what was prophesied – an angel has his foot on our rooftop saying VICTORY!

God has blessed me with a loving and caring husband as well as some dear sisters in Christ. I know that through it all, this too shall pass and will be just another chapter in the Book. God, give our family strength.

His promises will never fail. I had been told that I had stories within me which would encourage the Body of Christ in nations and generations to come. I was told that I would write books because I had books in me and my books would affect millions. It meant that there was a promise of life and strength to fulfill that purpose, and I had to grab a hold of that promise.

It amazes me at times when I go over my journals and read some of the entries; I would think how I prophesied to myself regarding this book in the midst of adversity. I would sit and just think about all the prophecies that I received over my life. As I read some of my older journals, I realize that I would not and could not die yet! I was like Simeon and Anna in the Bible. They had both received a promise that they would see the Messiah before they died. It meant that nothing could kill either of them until the promise had been fulfilled (Luke 2:25-38). As long as I have His promises over my life, NOTHING can kill me.

The prophecies that were spoken over my life have not been fulfilled yet. So I stood on the Word of God and would constantly repeat the prophecies to myself and speak life. I would say, "Just as You spoke to me before I was diagnosed, please speak to me again," and He would.

I wrote this book because I see my testimony bless so many people. I am thankful for the journal entries that are in this manuscript. There are many more books like this that are locked up inside me. They are just waiting to be manifested in their right season. My journal entry for May 30, 2010 reads:

Today is the day the LORD has made, I will rejoice and be glad in it. Church was good. Pastor Griffin prophesied and stated that I have to take this journey. I know that I have to but am I ready? No. But I know that with God and my family by my side, I will be all right.

Tomorrow is Memorial Day. We really don't have anything planned. I really want to show my mom a good time while she is here. I guess we'll find something to do. I really want to go take some family pictures.

Deodria (my baby sister) and Jakisha (my oldest daughter) will be up here to visit for a week. It's a shame that we have to wait for a life-threatening disease to hit our family before we visit each other or tell each other "I love You."

LORD, I know that I have some very big decisions to make. When they were about to leave, Jaz asked me if I will need them. I told her that I would rather for them (kids) not to see me go through the chemo ordeal. Ericka texted me stating that the dream she had meant that we will have a long journey, but we would be together throughout this journey.

That only confirmed what Pastor Griffin had prophesied to me today. LORD, just stay with me on this journey.

Was I prepared for this journey? Absolutely not! But I knew that I had a long battle ahead, and as long as the LORD is on my side, this is a journey worth taking. My journal entry for June 23, 2010 reads:

I went to a revival tonight. I had maybe three or four treatments and Prophet Butler, who had prophesied that an angel was on my rooftop proclaiming victory, had come to speak again.

This was the second time I was going to hear him preach. While he was in the middle of his preaching, he turned to me and said, "I don't know who you are but there are angels all around you. They are leaping up and down saying, "Healed! Healed!"

Nobody at that time knew I got diagnosed for I had not told anyone. It was through that episode that some people heard that I had cancer.

I went down and he said, "Bring her here." He started praying and when he finished, I said to him, "I was diagnosed with cancer." I got this all in video.

God had used him to give the prophetic word before I got diagnosed, that I would sit among kings and queens and that I had favor.

Diagnosis: Cancer

When I got that word from the LORD, that the angels said "healed," it held me through it all. Throughout all I experienced – the hospitalization, blood transfusion, infections and other complications – I held on to that prophetic promise.

It is really important to go back to the LORD and ask Him to give you a word when you are about to start at anything; a word which will make you hold on to Him.

Receive that word and it will undergird you especially in those low points in your journey where trials and temptations begin to buffet and threaten to pull you out of the redemptive course the LORD wants you to take.

In the Scriptures and even in these contemporary times, everyone who fulfilled his destiny was undergirded by prophetic promises. Undoubtedly, these prophetic promises will become the hedge that will keep you from falling away if you grab a hold of them in those dark stormy portions of your journey with the LORD.

CHAPTER ELEVEN

LIVING WITH AN ILEOSTOMY BAG

An **ileostomy** *is a surgical opening created by bringing the end or loop of small intestine (the ileum) out onto the surface of the skin. It is given when a tumor causes blockage in the colon or rectum. Intestinal waste traverses out of the ileostomy and is collected through an external pouching system stuck to the skin by a special clamp. Ileostomies are usually situated above the groin on the right hand side of the abdomen. Ileostomies are necessary where a disease or an injury has rendered the large intestine incapable of safely processing intestinal waste, typically because the colon has been partially or wholly removed. An ileostomy may also be necessary in the treatment of colorectal cancer*
(www.wikipedia.org/wiki/Ileostomy).

In some cases, the ileostomy is temporary as the common surgical procedure for colorectal cancer is to reconnect the remaining sections of the colon or rectum following the removal of the tumor, provided that enough of the rectum remains intact to preserve sphincter function. In a **temporary ileostomy**, a loop of the small intestine is brought through the skin, and the colon and rectum are not removed. When healing has happened, the temporary ileostomy is then taken down or reversed by surgically repairing the loop of intestine which made the temporary stoma, and closing the skin incision.

Diagnosis: Cancer

This was the case after my operation. Ileostomy is usually referred to as a BAG.

The tumor I had was not very low. It was on the colon, at the top of the rectum. When I had finished the twenty-eight rounds of radiation and five weeks of daily chemotherapy, I was to have surgery.

The after-effects of the intense therapy made me weak and nauseated. I did not go out in the daytime. The light and sun affected my system making me really nauseated, lightheaded and feverish whenever I would get exposed. I was told that my immune system was down.

For one month after therapy, I built up my immunity Levels and strengthened my body through healthy diet, rest and moderate exercise to handle the surgery. After weeks of daily, heavy doses of medication, a month of not taking anything but healthy food was bliss for my body. I was feeling so well that I did not want to think I was going to the hospital again.

When surgery time came, I put it off for another week because the spirit of fear was creeping in again. When the schedule for my surgery came up for the second time, I cancelled again and kept on shifting the surgery goal post.

Nevertheless, when I did call my doctor again two days prior to the postponed surgery, I asked him, "Is there any way I can push it back?" He encouraged me to go ahead with the surgery and get it over with.

Finally, the day of the surgery arrived and I was admitted for the procedure. I had lengthy conversations with my surgeon about the chances of me having a bag. He said that there was a fifty-fifty chance that I would need it. He told me, "I will not know whether you will need a bag until I open up your system and look at it." I was adamant and told him, "I better not wake up with a bag, Dr. Taylor."

He promised to do his best but could not guarantee that I would not require a bag. My final say was, "You are the best surgeon in the country; I better not wake up with a bag. I tell you Doctor, I don't want to wake up with a bag!"

He explained that if I did get a bag, it would not, thankfully, be a permanent bag. My tumor had not spread too low. He said, I would have a bag for only nine months at most, then he would do a reversal surgery. But I said to him, "I don't want a bag for two or three months. I just don't want a bag, period!"

My mother and Terrence were with me at the hospital. Bishop and Prophetess Franklin came all the way from Florida just to pray with me before the surgery. We had a wonderful time of prayer believing that I would not need the bag. I trusted that everything would be okay and the surgery would go without a hitch.

I went into surgery.

When I was brought to the recovery room, I woke up. The first thing I checked was for the dreaded bag.

I felt the bag.

Oh my goodness! I FLIPPED!

After surgery, the first bag that they would put on you is the standard hospital issue ileostomy which is quite long and bulky. The nurse tried to console me and tell me that I would be okay but I would hear none of it. I was really upset, completely inconsolable.

Waking up to see that a portion of my small intestine was out and that long bag attached to it, was REPULSIVE! I had heard about it but I had never seen it.

My next thought was, *I am better off dead!*

The doctor was quite happy with my healing process because during surgery, he found out that the tumor was completely gone. From an eight-centimeter cancerous lump to nothing in those few weeks was a great miracle. He said to us that it seemed that the radiation got it all. In retrospect, I know that Jesus had got it all, but at that moment, I was seeing RED!

The doctor explained that he had just gone in and cut off the portion where the tumor had been and it needed time to heal, uninterrupted by bowel movements. I was unimpressed. I was not interested in all that good news stuff right then! I did not want to hear that the tumor was gone or that there was no more cancer. I was UPSET because I HAD A BAG and I WANTED TO DIE!

I was like, *LORD, why did you allow me to have a bag? I had been married for only fourteen months. I am newlywed and now, I have a bag. How was this going to work with my husband?* My esteem was suddenly below zero and faith was out of the window that fast.

I was at the end of the journey and I wanted to give up; throw away every victory and wallow in a big ugly puddle of self-pity and RAGE!

I HAD A BAG!

Living With An Ileostomy Bag

Such a little thing had become the dark giant cloud that covered every other good thing. The Bible says:

The thief's purpose is to steal and kill and destroy. My purpose is to give them a rich and satisfying life.

—JOHN 10:10, NLT

I am sure the enemy was rolling on the floor with laughter. When he cannot kill or destroy you, he will look for all possible ways to steal from you.

I had successfully come to the end of the most difficult leg of the journey and I let *him*, the enemy, blow up a little thing and steal my joy. He was able to steal the recognition that the tumor that had given me misery for a long time; the thing I had prayed to be totally healed, had gone miraculously. I had no tumor, no cancer.

He was able to rubbish all of that for my want of *no bag*. Then, all I could see was *the bag* and every other victory was of no use at all.

It reminds me of Elijah on his journey to turn the hearts of Israel back to God (I Kings 17-18). He had a three-and-a-half year walk with the LORD which culminated in a most spectacular display of the LORD by answering Elijah's prayer through fire on Mount Carmel. Elijah had a great showdown with the prophets of the demon-god Baal and goddess Asherah. He had trounced those demons, killed their prophets and caused the entire nation to proclaim, "*The LORD, He is God!*"(I Kings 18:39).

After that victory, Elijah got a message from Jezebel, the wicked queen. She had no power of her own, but only usurps her

87

Diagnosis: Cancer

husband King Ahab's authority to push her agenda. She threatened Elijah that she would kill him.

Every miracle, every spectacular victory that Elijah had won for the past three-and-a-half years became nothing in his eyes because suddenly that puny little threat became the big giant. It stole every other joy of victory from him. The threat was all he could see. Elijah ran away, fearful and disgusted with himself that he was a failure. He wanted to die! (I Kings 19:1-5, 10).

But if not for the mercies of the LORD, this great prophet would have perished from A THREAT! Jezebel had not done anything and was not even able to do anything. Elijah had already forgotten that the same God, who had whisked him away and hid him from the king for all those years, could do it again.

The enemy could not undo the victory of turning the hearts of the people back to the LORD. He could not raise all the dead false prophets. The worst he could do was to make it a sour victory for Elijah and lie to him that he was a failure and all his service to the LORD was futile. He made Elijah think he was alone in his service to the LORD. The enemy blinded him from the reality that there were seven thousand others who had been faithful.

When we lose the joy of the LORD, we lose our staying power and the spirit of death quickly glides in. "The joy of the LORD is our strength" (Nehemiah 8:10). When you let go of joy, death sneaks in.

John the Baptist was not only a fearless prophet, but also a forerunner to prepare the way for the coming of Israel's Messiah, Jesus Christ. John the Baptist had lived an austere life and served the LORD wholeheartedly. For nine months, he was

The Voice in the Desert of Judea. He was recognized as the greatest Old Testament prophet. Jesus Christ Himself said, *"Among those born of women, no one is greater than John"* (Luke 7:28). John was faithful in his service; he spoke with fire and with power. He had a great following, yet, he submissively handed the baton of ministry to Jesus Christ after he had identified and baptized Him. When his disciples asked why he did this, John said *"He must increase and I must decrease"* (John 3:30).   What a humble servant of the LORD!

However, when Herod locked him up he became disillusioned. His disciples came to tell him about Jesus Christ's ever expanding ministry of power, miracles, signs and wonders. They had just witnessed Jesus raise from the dead the son of the widow of Nain.

As they shared these powerful testimonies, John was not listening. He could not see it. Instead, he sent his disciples to ask the LORD Jesus, "Are You the One [Messiah] or should we expect another?" That was a very telling statement.

It spoke volumes about his feelings of failure. He felt he had not ushered in the Messiah. He was no longer sure. His expectation had not been met. He was rotting in the dungeon and this supposed Messiah was not coming to his rescue. All his great successes had turned to ashes in the face of Herod's unjust incarceration (Luke 7:11-19). John was challenged to walk with a God he did not understand nor could predict, and he was in a dark place in the journey.

Was this the one about whom the angel had said to his father Zechariah, "He will be a joy and delight to you, and many will rejoice because of his birth?" John saw nothing delightful in and about his life right then. He had let the enemy steal his joy.

Diagnosis: Cancer

The enemy was able to steal that assurance that John had done his duty well. John was no longer sure that he had ushered in the right Messiah.

When the enemy fails to kill or destroy you completely, he will steal from you. The first thing he is capable of stealing is your joy and your confidence. If you are not careful, you will perish at of the point of your victory.

So there I was in the company of Elijah, John the Baptist and the countless others who nearly perished at the point of victory. I was so angry, shocked and disbelieving that I had to go around with this bag; death was a better deal.

Bishop and Prophetess Franklin, my mom and husband were on pins and needles. None of them could put a word in edgeways. Finally, my mom asked me, "How are you feeling?"

"I have a bag. How do you think I am feeling?" Everyone was quiet. They were scared to say anything. After that, Bishop Franklin said to me, "I got this teddy bear for you. I named her Miracle." I was like, "Mm hmm!" I shook my head and they rolled me into my room.

I lay there a complete sourpuss, frowning and nobody could say anything. My vibe was, LEAVE ME ALONE! They would ask, "You need anything?" "No."

Bishop and Prophetess had come all the way from Florida and I was spewing hostile vibes. They told me they had to go. I was glad and told them I wanted to be alone. Everyone could go because I did not want anyone and did not need anything. I HAD A BAG and that was more than I ever needed thank you!

Living With An Ileostomy Bag

No one even had a chance to make a thanksgiving prayer that the surgery was successful because at that point, I saw absolutely nothing to be thankful for.

GOD HAD GIVEN ME A BAG! That was NOT good! My marriage was going to be ruined and everything was going to be a mess!

In retrospect, I am so sorry about the terrible attitude I've shown to all those wonderful people who had come to be with me for support.

When everyone was gone, I went to sleep. That is when the LORD came to me in a dream. He was ANGRY! He asked, "How dare you? How dare you? You are alive and well and you complain about a bag?" The Bible says that it is a fearful thing to fall in the hands of the LORD. This wonderful loving Father Who can take a lot of our silly little idiocies does not raise spoilt brats.

I did not need further chastisement. That statement was enough. I woke up and my entire behavior changed. I repented for the bad attitude and thanked the LORD for all the healing. I embraced the bag and resolved that I would wear it with grace. So I called Prophetess Franklin and asked for my wig and make up. I was not going to let this bag change my life for worse. It was a challenge to be surmounted.

I asked for my computer to be brought to my hospital room and I began to search for a selection of smaller bags. I managed to get specialized smaller bags, but I would have to change them more often. I embraced it and determined to make the best of it.

From then on, I was around everyone every day. No one even noticed that I had a bag. I could dress up fashionably. I wore T-shirts, shorts and fitting clothes without anybody detecting that I had a bag. We went on vacations, on a cruise. I wore ball gowns, dresses, and no one had a clue I had a bag for nine months.

After the nine months recovery period, I was scheduled for a reversal surgery. That is where the surgeon withdraws the small intestine and reconnects it to the large intestine.

When I went before my close friends to tell them that I was going for a reversal, no one could believe that all that time, I had been using the bag. The LORD wanted me to experience everything that came with the medical treatment of that cancer so that I, too, could encourage others who may be stuck because they have a bag or do not think they could survive with one. He wanted to show me that I could have a full and amazing life with the bag.

It was not the end of the road. I have lived it and I know that as long as you hand it over to the LORD, you will not miss out on anything you desire to achieve in life, even with the bag. You don't have to miss out on anything because you have a medical gadget to aid you function as normally as possible.

CHAPTER TWELVE

OVERCOMING FRUSTRATIONS

Why me, LORD?

The LORD said to me in a loud audible voice, "Why not you?"

I was in the prayer closet. I had a prayer shawl that my daughter had made for me. During the night, I would wait till midnight, when everyone was asleep, to go and pray.

My husband would be asleep or downstairs and I would go and release my frustrations in the prayer closet with the LORD. I would cry and cry asking, "Why? Why? Why me?" And the LORD's response halted the waterworks right there! That was it. I dried my eyes out and realized I was going through that journey for a reason. This test was going to be my testimony.

During the first phase of treatment, I was like a caged person. I could not go anywhere and I let very few people know that I had cancer. I stayed in the house, prayed all day, read a lot, and listened to praise and worship. During that period, Juanita Bynum's worship music was a balm to my hurting soul. I listened to her a lot.

I was like the woman with the issue of blood. Her story is found in the book of Luke 8:43-45. She had spent twelve years in that condition. She had tried different doctors, different types of medication until she had exhausted all of her resources.

In ancient Israel, according to Moses' laws, a woman with an issue of blood could not mingle with other people. She was separated from society until the issue stops. That lady had been suffering in isolation for twelve years.

Women during their menstrual cycle could not mingle, eat or even share a seat with other people because they were ceremonially unclean. If she interacts with the people, she would bring defilement to them and cause the LORD to punish them. She had to hide her condition from as many as possible to avoid being stoned to death if she was caught in public (Leviticus 15:25-31).

She was desperately lonely. Even when she did gather her guts and go out to seek for help from the LORD, she had to sneak around, crawl on the ground so that she would not have any bodily contact with the crowd. That is why she said, "If only I could touch the hem of his garment, I shall be made whole." She was crawling through the crowd.

I felt like that woman. I could not go anywhere or speak to anyone about my condition. As it were, I hid it from as many as possible to avoid stones of negative words to be hurled my way. It was a very frustrating choice. However, the positive side of it was that my atmosphere was guarded. My spiritual space was always positively filled with the promises, praise and worship of the LORD.

Why me, LORD?

I felt frustrated when my treatment regimen started and I was alone. My husband was getting his car restored and the children were in Florida. Everyone was busy with their agendas and I, who was so used to multi-tasking, had to literally be still. The weakness, the tiredness, the inability to go out in the light was eating me away.

Overcoming Frustrations

My having two businesses is proof that I am used to working a lot. I had started initiatives in the city which had not been there before, but now, they are taking form. I had the first African American newspaper, the first African American business network in that city. Everything had been going very well. Then all of a sudden, I had to stop and shut down. I was a social person that was abruptly confined to one spot – indoors with minimal interaction with people.

My life took a hundred-and-eighty degree turn from very busy and social, to sedentary and isolated. But I spent those moments in prayer and listening to the LORD. I was frustrated because I had found the love of my life and now, I felt like a burden to him. We were just beginning to enjoy our lives when, Boom! It looked like everything was falling down around my ears.

Why me, LORD? What happened?

The LORD's constant refrain was, "Why not? If not you, then who?

I had to learn to keep an open ear that listens to what the LORD is saying and teaching me in each and every situation. I learned that I could use a frustrating situation to make a difference in other people's lives.

Life goes on even if I do not. I look back and see that my family, my friends, literally everyone was moving on without me.

I could have given in to my emotions, my flesh. I could have given up the fight because I am tired of this long-drawn-out treatment that has become a burden to my loved ones. I could have lay down my arms and quit struggling for my health and life. I could have surrendered and resolved to die.

Diagnosis: Cancer

My family would have found a way to adjust without me. Yes, they would suffer a great loss, but it would not stop their world. They would still live their lives. My children would have finished school and pursue their ambitions. My husband would have surely found a way to continue living. I would have become just a memory. That's good, but still a memory. The loss would not be on my family, the loss would be on me. I had to choose to either stand and be counted, or perish and disappear into the sands of time.

And if in case I went to be with the LORD, **would the nations and generations suffer a great loss from my absence here on earth?** Only the LORD and I would know. It would be a portion of destiny that nobody else could ever fulfill. They would never know what they missed. Only the LORD and I would know the loss if I refused to wrestle for my life and health out of the devil's clutches and overcome the frustrations and feelings of depression.

It is often said that the greatest talents, the best books, the most exciting movies and many record-breaking beats lay buried in cemeteries. It is true. Even before putting my story to paper, it had become a great inspiration and motivation to many people who have heard it. If I had decided to die, the world would never know what crucial portion they missed. The lives that were meant to be touched by my life story would operate with something missing. They would never even realize what a loss they had experienced. They would never be quite fulfilled without my little but vital portion added to their lives.

I chose to fight the fight of faith, and to take a positive attitude with the illness and its frustrations.

Overcoming Frustrations

I could still take the fresh breath of life despite the stench of death that came with cancer. The situation turned out to become a blessing, not only to me, but also to the businesses that were born out of this journey and to the many others who have encountered my story.

Living with the bag could be very frustrating. Once I put the bag on, the clamp would last for at least four to five days. At times, the clamp would need changing while we were out of town.

Once during Thanksgiving, we had gone to Fort Myers to be there with family. I had a diaper bag that I carried everywhere I went. It contained the extra bags for changing, cream, antiseptic and all the other medication I ought to have with me.

When I was due for a change, I realized that I did not have any more bags. We tried to call everywhere in Fort Myers, but they did not have them. I had started leaking and it was absolutely horrible even though the bag leaked for a really short time. So, I went all the way back home to Tampa, disappointingly, they too did not have any bags. However, they found a company where I could get them; it was a company in Riverview FL which is only fifteen minutes outside of Tampa. .

Every so often, the area on my stomach around the wound would get raw like a diaper rash. I would have to put alcohol on it for remedy.

Those were very frustrating times, so I looked forward to the reversal surgery. It is most convenient for my body to operate the way the LORD designed it. I could not wait to get *back to normal.*

Diagnosis: Cancer

The Reversal Surgery

I wish I had kept the bag!

I cannot imagine that the same Alicia who had griped and belly-ached about getting off the bag would ever think this way even for a moment! In my faith journey to health, I consider the initial effects of the reversal surgery one of the most frustrating events. What?!

For the nine months that I was using the ileostomy, I did not have my rectal sphincter muscles in use. They had a good holiday so they were completely relaxed. It meant that I was completely incontinent when I had the reversal. How frustrating and embarrassing can that get?

I got online to see what other people's experience had been, and sure enough, virtually everyone online was saying, "I wish I had kept my bag."

I would have eight to ten diarrheal moments a day. The most frustrating part was in that a week and a half after getting back home from the hospital; I had to take anti-diarrhea pills every day. I had to increase my intake of fiber. If I took any water, it would go directly through my system for I had no control. Unforgettable was the time when we went out to eat with my daughter. When we got home, I was lying down on her bed when all of a sudden I felt I had to go to the bathroom. Guess what? I did not make it. Jasmine had to help clean me up. I would cry out my frustration, *why is this happening to me?*

I would call my doctor because the stool was very loose. When I went to a restaurant or to a function, I would not drink anything at all, I would just eat.

Overcoming Frustrations

As I got used to my rectal functions again, with the changed diet and anti-diarrheal pills, I started the journey to full health. The doctors advised me that it would take around two years before my bowels get back to normal. I believe it was worth it. I would soon have the proper use of my body parts! I was eventually glad to have the reversal.

All illnesses are frustrating, but frustrations should not get you down. It should make you uncomfortable enough to refuse and resist that condition and get your health back from the devil.

For those who require a medical gadget to help them fully operate like pace-makers, hearing aids, ileostomies, wheelchairs, crutches or walking aides, and any other device, ask the LORD to help you embrace and adjust to it as far as He will let it happen.

Ask Him if it is a permanent set up because He is a God of impossibilities. You will receive your healing according to the measure of your faith and to His purposes for your own personal journey. Not everyone's experience is similar. Just hear Him and do what He tells you to do.

Ask Him to help you develop a full life despite that gadget. He is faithful. He is able to do many exploits through your experience. Let that frustration become the stepping-stone to your next level.

Diagnosis: Cancer

CHAPTER THIRTEEN

BATTLES WITHIN A BATTLE

Not only did my faith journey come with its frustrations, but there were a couple of real battles that had to be overcome also.

Christians have one big war with the kingdom of darkness but there are many battles within that war. When the enemy brings something in your life in order to steal from you, he will ultimately use it to kill and destroy you. When he wants to bring death in your life, he will try to create an entrance using the other areas of your existence through which he can pass. Therefore, when you roll over with the punches he is administering, you are helping him open the doors even wider and make huge inroads into your life.

When I became unwell, the enemy was not only going to attack my health, but he was also out to get every other part of my life and destroy all of them until nothing remained. He fights dirty. He was out not only to kill me with cancer, but also to kill my marriage, children, and businesses and leave nothing remaining. If I succumbed to his attacks and let my emotions dictate how I operated, then, I would have been destroyed long time ago.

However, I know that the LORD Jesus Christ already warned that in this world, there would be many tribulations, but we were to be of good cheer because He had overcome the world (John 16:33). Therefore, all I had to do was come and collect the pickings. Jesus Christ had made me more than a conqueror and a winner before I even step into the battle arena. He won two thousand years ago and it was up to me to make that provisional truth into a conditional reality in every aspect of my life.

My children were brought down to Fort Myers for the summer vacation. I had been undergoing treatment for about a month and my body was beginning to really succumb to the therapy. At that low point, I remember receiving a phone call informing that Ladarris had been arrested. I collapsed and began to cry. I told the LORD, "I am not there. My son is with his biological father and he is not much of a role model. His father lets him have his way down there. Let nothing happen to my son down in Fort Myers. Don't kill him LORD. Let nothing happen to him."

God said very clearly, "I did not kill him." At that time, I did not know what the LORD meant. I stopped crying and started praising Him.

Later on, I found out that he and some boys were chased by the police and my son jumped into a canal and began to drown. Somehow, he managed to get out. Ladarris was arrested and was later sent to prison. That is when I knew what the LORD had meant when He said "I did not kill him." The LORD actually saved my son's life.

Before I relocated from Florida to Alabama, I operated a business with another lady friend. When I left Florida, she continued running the business which was a mortgage real estate and tax company. During my time of illness, she called me and said we were being investigated by the Internal Revenue Services. They were going to carry out an investigative audit on our activities for the duration of the company's existence. They scrutinized every single file we had. It was a very harrowing battle on top of the battle that I was facing with my health.

Another battle came through the medical insurance company. Even though I was approved for medical insurance just as I began the treatment, the insurance company said they did not know if they would pay for the medical bills stemming from the cancer therapies. I went to the doctor but they were on hold for payment. They tried to claim that I had a pre-existing condition.

My godmother worked in an insurance company and had been the first African American who was the overall department head in New York. I had received insurance coverage in the beginning of May 2010 and in about two weeks; I was diagnosed with cancer. She said to me that if they granted that insurance, it would be a miracle. It was very dicey on their part if they would pay.

It became another prayer point on my ever-lengthening list before the LORD. I said, "LORD, let my file get into the hands of a Christian. Allow whoever gets my file to give me divine favor." After about a month, the insurance company began to pay the bills and I had insurance cover for the duration of my treatment. Like my godmother said, it definitely was God stepping in because it was not humanly possible.

The battle with idleness confronted me. What was I to do with all these hours in the house? The two new ventures I had initiated when we first moved to Alabama had closed down when I was just about to take off, about to begin creating my niche within the business union in our town.

Diagnosis: Cancer

I was enjoying the busyness, the people whom I had hired and those whom we had begun to network with at First Fridays' Networking. It was a battle to choose solitude and seclusion over that full life.

Sometimes, prayer, reading the Scriptures and staying connected with the LORD was a battle in itself especially on those days when it was generally uncomfortable; those days when the fever fluctuated and I was confined in the hospital.

It was a battle I had to overcome because I knew that I was only going to get my healing through prayer. What you get by prayer, you keep by prayer. I learned to pray, read the Bible, and worship in season and out of season.

In that season, it was not just cancer that the enemy used to fight with me. He tried to punch from every direction. I often wondered what was going on. The refrain was, "Why me? And the LORD would reply, "Why not you?"

I wrestled with my emotions so many times. I struggled with the idea that I may be a burden to Terrence. Here he was expecting to enjoy marital bliss and what was he getting? *An invalid wife?*

It was a battle and at that point, many marriages do crumble and do not quite recover. It is at these times that a spouse or a member of the family may decide that he is better off dead than become a burden. When one makes a decision to give up when passions are running all over the place because of battles and frustrations, it is a subtle form of committing suicide.

The LORD has given us a free will. There is no way that He takes away people before their time. It is a choice they make. Even though Jesus Christ knew He was meant to die for the sins of man, He still had a choice to take that cup or leave it. He has the choice to live, marry and have a family. The freedom to choose is never taken away from any of us because the LORD would be violating His gift of a free will.

It is the devil that coerces a person into a particular kind of decision. He does not allow you to make free and good choices. He will stir up your emotions, kick up dust, make you see that you are a burden then lead you to your death.

The enemy will make you feel you are doing the right thing in just letting go and dying. Like I mentioned before, the LORD will not punish you or reject you for choosing death. However, you and many others lose something vital in their destiny when you let your emotions dictate your choices.

It was in that season of battles and frustrations that I learned the power of emotions; how to harness them and bring them to subjection. It is at those hotspots in the journey that I could have chosen to die because the frustrations and battles that came with the illness stirred up strong negative emotions.

When I thought I might be a burden to my husband and family, I had to declare and proclaim who I am in God and my destiny in Him. I was His burden and He was more than able to carry me through. I spoke to the demonic forces and let them know that I believed the report of the LORD. I rebuke them so that they could not use my flesh and soul to destroy me. Life was on my tongue. It was my choice and I constantly fought that battle.

Those battles were all part of subduing my flesh to enable me to hear the LORD moment to moment about each situation. In those times, I did not **follow my heart** because the Bible says *"The heart is deceitful above all things and beyond cure. Who can understand it?"* (Jeremiah 17:9).

The heart is the seat of our emotions. I dared not trust mine especially when they lead me to thoughts that were contrary to the LORD's purposes. It was in those moments that I realized the importance of hearing the still, small voice of the LORD in the midst of the battles and choosing His way over mine; no matter how noble and good my way sounded in my ears.

When it came to the battle with my esteem as a marital bed-partner, I had to pray and cast out those feelings of inadequacy as a wife especially after I went through the surgery. When I first came home from the surgery for maybe a week or so, my husband and I would try to get intimate and he could not. He made a mistake, rubbed the bag, and asked me to give him some time because of the bag. I rolled over and started crying. *LORD, how will I do this? My husband is not going to make love to me anymore because I have a bag. O my God, what is going to happen to my marriage? God, you said marriage is honorable and the bed is not defiled. How will this work?*

I cannot explain what happened but I just had an assurance that the LORD would work it out.

After that incident, we enjoyed the most joyful intimacy from that time on. I talked about it with him one time and wondered what changed. He said to me, "You know it came to a point where the bag was not even a problem. I did not realize you had a bag." I would ask him how he felt about my illness. He says, "Alicia, your cancer treatment went so quickly. It seemed as if you got diagnosed yesterday, got treatment and surgery today. It went by so quickly."

The Bible says that our times are in the LORD's hands (Psalm 31:15). While I thought the treatment was so long and traumatic over those many months, the LORD simply fast-forwarded the same time span for my husband. He thought it went like a breeze. It was the LORD's doing and it was marvelous in my eyes.

I had expected to receive instantaneous healing. Yet, He let me walk through the entire medical process. Through every step, the LORD was revealing to me that when He had prescribed the cure, He would ensure that everything else that seemed impossible to man would fall into place, even the sense of time span for my husband. My intimacy with my husband was a major case in point. We overcame that battle even without my realizing it.

My self-image was a battle. No matter how bad I felt, I was fashionable. I wore different hairstyles and dressed up a lot. I bought head wraps to match my dresses. When I went to the Cancer Center, they commented that I always looked very well dressed that was generally so nice.

I make sure I was well dressed whenever I went out in public. I did not want anyone to know I have cancer. I wanted to look as normal as possible even when I did not feel beautiful. I wore make-up and was well put-together. I refused to look sick or frumpy at all. Refusing to look like what the circumstances said about me was in a way a statement of faith. I was going to look like what God said I looked like – beautiful, healthy and above reproach.

The battle went beyond battling self-esteem. The LORD does not want us to have self-esteem. His will is for us to have **God-esteem**.

When our esteem comes from knowing who we are in Him, then it does not matter what we say about ourselves, or what other people say about us. It does not matter what the medical professionals say about us or what the world says about

Diagnosis: Cancer

us. We are esteemed highly by Him no matter our circumstances may be.

As long as I walk in obedience to the LORD, as long as I remain on the course He has set for me, then He becomes my esteem standard. He will always remain in high-esteem, faultless and perfect. The Bible underlines this fact:

Yet now He has reconciled you to Himself through the death of Christ in His physical body. As a result, He has brought you into his own presence, and you are holy and blameless as you stand before him without a single fault.

—COLOSSIANS 1:22, NLT

I got acquainted with some people in the clinic. It's amazing how the LORD seemed to have someone prepared to encourage me with a word.   Others uplifted me through their own stories of faith as they walked their own journey to health.

I see people get surprised whenever I tell them that I, too, was sick. I never knew who I would meet every day, so I would always try to drop nuggets of encouragement and faith. I overcame the battle with godly-esteem by seeking to encourage others and look like how the LORD said I looked.

Wherever you see the word faith in the Bible, look around at the stories around it and you will see a struggle of some sort. We are exhorted to fight the good fight of faith (1
Timothy 6:12).

Battles Within A Battle

It is a battle to stand in faith. The enemy will try to throw everything at you to stir up your emotions especially when you are going through a low or weak season. Emotions can start all kinds of physical and spiritual battles, and if you give in, remember that the chain will always break at the weakest link.

That is his strategy – to weaken you so that he can steal your joy and strength with it. Then in that weak disposition, he will fight you with other opportunistic circumstances and eventually destroy you.

Never give up.

Do not let your emotions dictate your circumstance. Fight, fight, and fight back. Reject negative emotions and hold on to whatever will lift your spirit. It is necessary to cut off any fuel that the enemy may use to attack you. Keep the faith.

These are but a few of the numerous little battles I encountered during my faith journey to health. I am sure that there will be more as the LORD moves me from glory to glory, from victory to victory.

Diagnosis: Cancer

CHAPTER FOURTEEN

STEPPING OUT ON FAITH

I must note that after the first round of radiation and chemotherapy, I really got to appreciate a life without medication. My body felt so happy for the one month of rest preceding the first surgery. Truly, health is wealth.

It is my prayer that you, my reader, will prosper in your health above everything else, and lead a lifestyle that will require no constant medication in Jesus' name. Amen.

After the tumor was surgically removed and the ileostomy installed, I must take on seven more rounds of aggressive intravenous chemotherapy to wind up the treatment and to ensure that there were no more cancer cells floating in my system.

I went to the Cancer Center and had a pump put in me so that the medication could be propelled into my body. Since the first five-week chemo session had not been so aggressive, I was not worried at all. I just knew that this, too, would be easy on my system.

I had to spend four hours at the Cancer Center for the chemotherapy session. After that, they left the pump in me so that I could go home with the medication continually pushing inside my body for the next forty-six hours. I was very well when I got home, that was not bad at all. I figured I could do this. We finished what was left of the day and went to sleep.

The next morning I woke up and was extremely ill. I had absolutely no strength to even lift an arm. I could not move or

111

get out of bed. I was so weak. Terrence was shocked at the change and prepared some food for me. I literally had to slowly crawl to use the bathroom. It was the worst feeling ever. This chemotherapy was no child's play. It was hard on my system.

I spent a day and a half in bed.

The next week, I was due for another chemo session. I did not go. I just could not bring myself to do it. I was thinking, LORD, I need a miraculous touch of healing. Do I have to endure six more sessions of horrible illness? The week after, I was supposed to go to the Cancer Center but baulked again. The doctor called me and so I told him that I did not want to do it because of how bad I felt. He said that they could lower the treatment dosage. So, they lowered my dosage and took the pump off. I still got very sick but not as bad as before.

Because of the side effects of the chemo regimen, I could not drink or eat anything cold at all. I could not get near a refrigerator because the coldness makes me feel like I was being cut by razor blades inside. I had to wear socks and gloves because my toes and hands were numb. I was not allowed to get under the sun too because of its effects on the medication in my system.

After the second treatment, I was still weak but I did not stay in bed. After they removed the pump, I felt really ill. I was able to go to four chemo sessions out of the seven, and then, I discerned that it was time to stop. I was completely healed. I believed God had given me my healing. I never took another treatment.

That was my first giant step of faith.

Stepping Out On Faith

From the time I received the diagnosis to the time I went in for reversal surgery, I had been undergoing treatment for fifteen months already. They did not remove the pump-port right then because they wanted to be sure that if they needed to give me more medication, the pump was already in me.

The doctor started with CAT scans and blood work. They carried out x-rays and other procedures, but all of them showed up clear – no cancer. Since that time up to the publication of this book, my health has been improving. I praise the LORD for total healing.

Since then, I was put on a clinical trial which they call *Quality of Life Trial*. Basically every six months, I have to take the CAT scans and blood work, and so far, it has continually been clear.

My next step of faith was returning to Florida. I was raised in Florida and my husband was from Alabama. When we got married, we went to Alabama and it was there where I was diagnosed. It was also there where I started my treatment.

After knowing that I had to get the aggressive chemo after the first surgery, we moved back to Florida because I did not have enough people with me for the support I needed in Alabama.

So, I was back to square one – having no business prospects, adjusting to living with the bag and undertaking the final round of chemo treatments. Thankfully, I was getting my health and strength back and was able to get out and about once more.

What to do?

During those days when I attended the first rounds of radiation and chemotherapy, I would get acquainted with the

113

people at the Cancer Center who looked very ill. Their hairs were in different stages of hair loss, so a number of the ladies had drab, sad looking headgears. The LORD planted the seed for a business idea which could also be ministry to cancer patients.

Once I was strong enough, I began to research and talk to a few people around Tampa about setting up business ventures that would serve the vision that the LORD has put in my heart. That was my third step of faith. I set up two businesses and they have been operating since the time they opened.

I was back on my feet and busy working on my businesses, only this time, they are coupled with a ministry to those undergoing health and other challenges. As I took little steps of faith, my test was beginning to become a testimony. What the enemy started to be a mess in my life was now developing into my message.

CHAPTER FIFTEEN

TRAGEDY TO TRIUMPH

Those bald-heads, turbans, and headscarves!

I had seen enough of them to last me a lifetime. Even up to this day, every time I see those head scarves tied in a distinct way, I just think, cancer!

When my treatment regimen began, I expected that all my body hair will fall off literally. So, I had prepared all kinds of wigs and make up and I would wear them. People asked about my hair at the Cancer Center. They would wonder, "It's not falling off. Your hair is beautiful." I reassured them that it was only because I purchased it.

Those experiences birthed one of my ventures, Pretty Laces ,Pretty Faces. I took my tragedy with cancer and went to train in Make-Up Artistry. I then developed the business name and partnered with Missy Lavette Johnson.

I had seen what other people with cancer went through: the loss of hair, the loss of esteem, and the emotional blow it could cause on a person's appearance, especially the ladies. I saw what alopecia can do to people.

Alopecia is a type of hair loss that occurs when your immune system mistakenly attacks hair follicles, which is where hair growth begins. It makes you bald, and sometimes you lose all body hair.

I developed a burden to make their experience better and help them turn it around and make a statement against what the enemy was trying to do to them. I understand the power of beauty and its ability to build esteem and make a statement of faith against what the circumstances were saying. We encourage people who come to our salon and help them transform the way they looked. It goes a long way in building hope, focusing on life and living it to the fullest. We have an annual *Strutting for a Cure Wig and Fashion Show* to raise funds for patients' wigs and hairpieces.

On Mother's Day 2013, we gave away free makeovers and wigs for cancer, alopecia and other patients that are suffering from hair-loss due to medical or hereditary issues. We always invite anyone who would like to donate to our patients to send their information to us. Our contacts are included in Appendix III.

Our tag-line is, *Bringing Out the You that You Never Knew.* On our logo we have faces. We also got a T-shirt called I am a Pretty Face. The philosophy behind these statements is: *It doesn't matter if your hair falls out or you lose your eyebrows or lashes, you still have a pretty face.* There is no real challenge, nothing difficult at all in transforming your total look. You just need to always remember, **you have a pretty face.** I took all the pain I had experienced and turned it into gain. That was the LORD's doing and it continues to be marvelous in my eyes.

My late great grandmother used to make an all-natural organic herb and oil grease for hair. I used it while undergoing chemo and amazingly, none of my hair shed off. Now, my cousin makes the grease and we sell it at the salon. We use it on our clients and their hair has either reduced shedding or grows.

Even though I cut my hair after the chemo because I had some thin spots, my hair grew well with the help of that hair product. Because of its success in keeping my hair quite strong, we set out to develop it as our own beauty item for a wider market. That, too, became another product of my tragedy.

Tragedy To Triumph

The second business I developed was Bethel *Business Solutions*. The LORD had me awake for two consecutive Mondays and told me how to go about this particular business. He gave me the name and the strategy for outreach. *Bethel Business Solutions is* a business mentorship program that helps people to start up their businesses.

I share my own business stories in the context of the tragedy of my illness, and how I was able to pick myself up again with the LORD's help. My main audience started within the church where people from all walks of life attended.

We teach people to step out in faith and start up new ventures. Then we equip them   from corporation to website development, marketing, and networking. We show them the possibilities of moving from a place of financial difficulty to a point of abundance through entrepreneurship.

I connected with a couple of coaches who helped mentor and develop me for the business world. I, in turn, mentor others and minister to them through principles in the Word of God. This particular business involves quite a bit of public speaking which the LORD is using to build my platform for the next level He has been preparing for me.

I don't know what the future holds, but I am excited about it because I know the LORD Who holds that future holds me too. Therefore, I am secured that in every portion of this journey, He will lead and guide me as long as I stay on course and walk in obedience to His will.

Diagnosis: Cancer

CHAPTER SIXTEEN

FAITH IS A LAW

I shared, at length, on faith in Chapters Five and Six. As I come to this leg in my faith journey, I would like to reiterate that faith is not a feeling. It is a real substance.

We are surrounded by an untold number of invisible forces and signals that we cannot see or hear with our eyes and ears: radio waves and cell phone transmissions, TV and cable broadcasts, infrared and microwaves, among many others. They have always existed and were very real before their miraculous discovery by man; before the invention of the radio, mobile phones, television and microwave oven. Without a doubt, there are many more amazing invisible physical forces that we have not yet discovered.

The same is true with the law of faith and the things of the spirit. You may not see them with your natural eyes, but they are there now, and they are very real. Through the Word of God, you can begin to unlock those spiritual laws which have hitherto been hidden by the circumstances that surround you.

Every law must have unchanging, non- negotiable principles that will make it operate. Basically in the law of gravity, if you jump off from a building in Tokyo, Florida or Cairo, you will fall to the ground. It does not change because you are rich, poor, tall or short, or are put together in a certain way. Unless a superior opposite law overrules the natural law of gravity, things will always be pulled downward.

A fully loaded cargo jet, or a massive Space Shuttle with its mammoth tanks and rockets at a total combined weight of two thousand tons, can defy the law of gravity and soar into the

119

sky at breathtaking speeds. How? By the application of higher laws and forces that overrule the natural law of gravity: The laws of AERODYNAMICS, the laws of thrust and lift.

Faith is a spiritual law and the Law of Faith supersedes or overrules EVERY NATURAL AND PHYSICAL LAW! It can turn things that seem impossible to the natural mind, a possibility.

The law of faith is undergirded by principles. It took learning those principles to walk in this journey. I did not know it all when I began, but I was learning as I walked. As I made mistakes in some areas and had success in others, I continue to learn.

Once those principles are in place, then they simply activate the law. It is an ongoing journey. I apply the law of faith to those principles that apply in any area of life. These are some of the principles which are found in the Faith Hall of Fame – the book of Hebrews chapter 11:

1. **The Principle of Existence** - You must believe that God is. It takes faith to believe in His existence just the way you believe that there are invisible forces or signals in microwaves or radio waves. You see their impact on technology, and in that same way, you will see the LORD's impact on all of creation on a daily basis.

2. **The Principle of Just Providence** – I shared concerning God's Providence in my own faith journey. He rewards those who diligently seek Him. I have tested this and proven that, indeed, He is a Just Rewarder.

3. **The Principle of the Invisible** - You must be prepared to believe in things beyond the reach of your five senses and emotions. You must believe in things that have never happened before in your world.

4. **The Principle of Future Preparation** – Ephesians 2:10 say that, "We are His workmanship created for good works which He had prepared in advance for us to do." You must believe that God's working for your good even before you knew Him or chose to make Him your LORD simply because He loved you and brought you into this world (Jeremiah 29:11; Philippians 1:6).

5. **The Principle of Endurance** – Hope that is generated from faith is what gives us the staying power, the ability to wait patiently through every high and stormy circumstance. It is the anchor that keeps our soul steadfast in the LORD because most of the time, our timing is not His. So, endurance keeps you patient with His timing. He knows when it is the right time for every need to be supplied.

6. **The Principle of Assured Conviction** – Paul said, "I know whom I have believed, and I am persuaded that He is able to guard that which I entrusted to Him until that day" (2 Timothy 1:12). It means linking the LORD's world-view to your own so that you can see things through His eyes. When you do that, you will see every mountain-sized problem as a mere speck in the eyes of the LORD. You will know that He has given you all things for life and godliness to flatten every mountain, raise every valley, straighten every crooked path, and even out every rough road. You will see every adversary as a friend and you can treat him well because you are convinced that everything is

under His control. You will look at your difficult circumstance and will know that it will turn around because He holds everything in His hand.

7. **The Principle of Incomplete Knowledge** – This means that you have an assurance and complete conviction that the LORD is in control. You do not have to know where exactly He is taking you. You do not need to have complete knowledge of the every detail of your life because you have faith and trust in Him who holds the details and knows everything. So, when He leads you to step out in faith, you simply step even though you do not know whether the bridge will appear only when you have lifted your foot towards a cliff. Abraham went out not knowing where he was going, but he knew who was going with him.

8. The **Principle of Reliance on Rhema** – Rhema is the specific word, the prophetic promise that the LORD releases once you step into the course of destiny. You should never leave home without it. Abraham believed God's personal rhema on him and it was counted to him as righteousness.

9. **The Principle of Heavenly Ambition** - Everything you do or experience has eternal consequences and you will answer for all of it one day. When you understand this principle, you will be careful how you handle your relationships and how you talk because every word that you uttered and every work you've done when no one is watching will be judged. This will increase your level of integrity and faithfulness. Faith is directed into God's purposes and to God's ends. It cannot function properly if it's focused on the here and now. Faith seeks the city that is to come.

10. **The Principle of Possibility** – Faith dictates that when we have exhausted all our human efforts and intellect seeking all possible solutions, faith kicks in to do the impossible and make it possible. When I was diagnosed with cancer, the medics did all they possibly could, but it was the LORD who made the cure possible. He shortened my treatment regimen. Not only did He resurrect my businesses, but He also gave a ministerial purpose that drives the businesses I run. He revived my marriage when I thought it would be impossible. Believe that, your impossible situation is possible with God. That is the victory that will overcome your world... even your faith (1 John 5:4-5).

11. **The Principle of Renunciation** – I shared how I deliberately decided to take steps that controlled my atmosphere. I did not let any negative utterance remain undealt with. I diffused every ill-spoken word of disease, death, and destruction with positive words of life, joy, peace, and healing. Faith operates in renouncing all that is non-faith and holding on to God's purposes ONLY. This is more so when you proclaim the prophetic word of the Scriptures. When you renounce every negative and anti-God statement and weed out from your vocabulary those words that reflect negativity, then your faith will be uncontaminated by the pursuits of this world.

12. **The Principle of Conquest** – We are encouraged by the words, "This is the victory that overcomes the world, even our faith." Faith is about being more than a conqueror or an overcomer because the LORD Jesus Christ had already overcome the world. Nothing in this existence can overcome us when we are walking in obedience to the LORD. Faith is external in conquering Canaan and internal in resisting temptation,

persecution and trials and testifying to God. Faith does not submit to circumstances but uses those circumstances as stepping stones to the next level of conquest.

I continue to make these principles my guiding compass in this faith journey. I continue to learn to operate by faith, and take each of these principles to make them my lifestyle. As you apply these principles too, may the Law of Faith in your journey supersede every other law that has hitherto hindered you or held you captive to a life that is not as full and satisfactory as the LORD intended for you.

CONCLUSION

My faith journey continues.

As we drove back home from yet another meeting where I shared my testimony and the lessons I learned from it, I reflected on the wonderful impact it had on my hearers.

I lifted up my eyes and continued to thank the LORD for my improving health on the journey thus far traveled. With the LORD on my side, I am excited about the future. I know that challenges lay ahead and therefore, greater triumphs. Truly, I have experienced the angel of the LORD declaring victory over my life.

Granted this is an ongoing journey. I don't know when it shall end, for there had been many dynamics to it.

Look on how the LORD dealt with Elijah: He told Elijah to go to the brook Cherith and stay there for a season, afterwards, the LORD again told Elijah to move down to Zarephath and live with a widow and her son.

The journey with the LORD is never one long, straight, boring path. It has many changes, and I continue to learn to have a listening ear. I believe that this has been part of the bigger journey in the making of a woman of God.

My journey is not too different from the exodus of the children of Israel when they were delivered from bondage in Egypt by the LORD's mighty Hand.

From Egypt, it was that same God who sent them, not to a lush green meadow, but to a wilderness where they were completely exposed to the elements in a scorching, waterless desert with scorpions and poisonous snakes. Yet in that desert, for forty long years, the LORD provided everything they needed. For forty long years, He was training a motley band of former slaves and transforming them into a formidable kingdom of faith-filled and revered priests and feared warriors. He transformed them to become His priests and kings that will serve as an example to the nations all around them.

He was training them to live, not by bread alone but by every word that proceeded from the mouth of the LORD. He was training them to live according to the laws of faith. It was not easy. Yet because Israel finally yielded to Him, He brought them into the Promised Land where they continued to learn.

Today, more than 3500 years later, even though some of the descendants of Israel did not pursue their faith in the LORD, Israel remains a feared, powerful nation surrounded by many enemies and but still capturing the world's attention in many ways.

As I step out of the car and thank the LORD for another fruitful day at work, I think, this link between the exodus and my own journey has an interesting connection. Maybe this could be the subject of another publication in my on-going faith journey.

ACKNOWLEDGEMENTS

No one walks alone in this journey called life, and for this reason, the Lord has poured wonderful people into my journey. They are mighty men and women of God to walk beside and behind me, extending help along the way. My deepest appreciation goes out to these exceptional few who served as my inspirations in writing this book:

To Lily Mudasia. A special thank you for your insight and wisdom. Your years of experience made this dream come to reality. You're the best!

To Wendy Walters and the Release the Writer Alumni. Thank you for being obedient to the voice of the Lord. The *Release the Writer Seminar* literally changed my life. My fear of writing was conquered and I stepped out in faith. Not only did I come out excited, but I also came back equipped as an author. Thanks for your prophetic words and for believing in me and *Diagnosis: Cancer.* You are such an inspiration to many.

To my staff at Bethel Business Solutions and Alicia Productions staff to say you're the best is an understatement. Colleen, thanks for keeping me on track and organized, Andrea, Felenna, DJ and Amber for all the phone calls and research. Thanks to each of you for making this happen. As I've stated before, "It's not about having a BIG team, but it's about having a GOOD team that works in unity and love." The best is yet to come.

To my Pretty Laces, Pretty Faces Staff Trina, Jakisha and Palik thanks for the love and support. I love you.

To Pastor Eric and First Lady Pamela Griffin. Thank you for everything. It was your love and support during that dark season of my life that kept a smile in my heart. First Lady Pam and thanks for not getting aggravated with all the calls and medical questions I had. You two are the best. Y'all will always be my Pastors and First Lady. I love you !

To Bishop and Prophetess Tiffany Franklin. Thank you for being in the midst of it all. From the operating room to the chemo treatment room, you were there. It was your prayers, late night conversations and inspiring words that truly anchored me to His promises.

To Pastor Gregory and Co-Pastor Marjorie Ford. Thank you for believing in me and the gifts that the Lord has bestowed upon me. You were always there for me. I love you.

To my sister and friend, Co-Pastor Timeko Whitaker. Thank you for your encouraging words and belief in me.

To the staff of John Amos Cancer Center: Dr. Pippas thank you for your sense of humor and of course those bow ties! (smile). No matter how bad it may feel or look, you always seem to bring a smile to my face.

Ms. Angela, ARNP, thank you for your kind words and sincerity. I will always remember how You helped me get assistance for my chemo medication right on my first doctor's appointment. You always called to check on me as if I was, as you would say, "missing". It is nurses like you that bring a ray of sunshine in a rainy day.

Mrs. Mary, RN, thank you for assisting me while I was fighting a battle within the battle. Thank you. You are one of the best clinical trial nurses around. God bless you.

To the staff of St. Francis Surgical Center: Dr. Taylor for being the best surgeon in the world, even after I woke up and seen the bag, and Ms. Lisa, RN, for helping me during my post-surgery recovery period. Thanks to the both of you.

Diagnosis: Cancer

To all my destiny helpers, Brenda Young , Nikia Toney, Sharon Adams, Ebony Brown, Tiki, Mother Jones,

My cousins, Sharon, Ann, Bonnie, and August. Thanks for traveling many miles to care for me after my surgery.

To my Aunts, Nieces, Nephews and all my In laws. Tonya I just want to thank you for everything you do.

To Grandma Dorothy Smith. Thanks for my *God answers Prayers* pillow. I still have it with me. I love you,

To my Apostle La Juan and Prophetess Valora Cole. Thank you so much for all the love and support. I will never forget that day when I was on the plane headed to the writers' retreat and the Lord spoke to me and said, "I have given you shepherds after My Own heart." I can truly say that the two of you are the genuine definition of love. I love you both so much and I am forever grateful.

To my Perfected Love International Fellowship (PLIF) family, I love you all.

To my M&M's: Missy Johnson and Maria Ramos-Person. Missy my Friend, Partner, and Sister. Thank you for being the definition of a true friend your encouraging words, advice and prayers. You just don't know how much you mean to me. I thank God every day for placing you into my life. Maria, I thank you for the love and support. I recall us riding in the back seat of the car and you stating *"When are you going to write that book?"* It was friends like you and Missy that pushed me to write. I sometimes sit back and think about how the Lord spoke to each of us at *Woman, Thou Art Loose Conference* in Atlanta last year. It is so amazing to see it all come to pass right in front our eyes.

Thanks for all the love and support. I love you my M&M's. The best is yet to come.

To my husband, lifelong partner and friend, Terrence, who is also affectionately known as my Hubby. Thank you for being there from the diagnosis, to the treatments, to the surgeries and prognosis. From the day we said, "I Do," and swore, "For better or for worse, in sickness and in health," you have truly lived out those vows. If I don't say it enough, now, I am telling you and the entire world that I love and appreciate you, Hubby.

To all my sons, daughters, and Godchildren, Ceedrick, Jakisha, Sa'Shae, Jacara, NaKelia, LaDarris, TerQuan, Jasmine, Terrence, Tar'Rence, Tre'Varius, and Rah'Jai. You all mean so much to me. I thank God for placing each of you in my life.

To my First Born Ceedrick Jr, I just want to thank you for traveling up to Georgia just to see me after my reversal surgery. Its moments like that I cherish the most. I love you Son.

To my little flower, Jasmine, that has blossomed into a young lady. Thank you my baby girl for the prayer shawl that you personally had made for me. It was during those profound prayer times that I would wrap up in that shawl and cry out to the Lord. I thank God for you.

To Nakelia, thank you for the flower. When you came in that hospital room after my surgery, it was a very lonely and down time for me. Your visit and that flower meant a lot. Blood could not make us closer.

To my daughter, friend, and right hand, Jacara. Thank you for always being there whenever I call. At times, I don't know what I would do without you. Not once did you complain, murmur, or groan. Instead you made yourself always available for me. Blood could not make us any closer. And like what I always say, "You are my little, mini me."

To my sister and God-sisters, De'Odria, Tamara, and Ericka, I love you all so much.

Tamara, thank you because from the time you entered into my life, you have been more than just a sister. You have been my friend, advisor and confidant. I can't wait to work with you side-by-side every day. I love you so much and I know that our best days are ahead of us.

Ericka, thank you for being my sister, nurse and friend. I look back over our lives and see how much we have been through together from childbirths, graduations, and sicknesses. But through it all, we always had each other. I am so proud of you and all your accomplishments. As little girls, we never thought our journey would be like what it is. I love you Ericka Small, MSN, ARNP, NP-C.

To DeOdria my baby sister/daughter. I sit back sometimes and look at the amazing lady you have become. I love you little sister.

To my mother, Cynthia Gibbs-Hampton. Thank you for being right by my side from the time you received the phone call. Growing up, I never understood why you were so strict. But now being a mother myself, I understand and appreciate the strictness because it made me into the woman that I am today. I love and appreciate you, Mother. I thank God for you.

To Mama A, This is a bitter sweet moment for me. I miss you so much. I know that you would be so proud of me. I don't know how I would have made it without you by my side. You always made yourself available for me. Not once did you ask for me to assist with airfare etc. You was just there. I learned so much from you. You helped mold me into the business woman I am today. Everything you did for me I am so grateful. I love and miss you so much Mama A.

To my grandchildren everything I do, I do for you. As the Bible states in Prov 13:22 "A Good man leaves an inheritance for his children's children. I am determined not to only leave an inheritance but a Legacy.

Most of all, to my sweet Lord and wonderful Savior, JESUS CHRIST. It is by Your Grace and Mercy that I am still here today. In Your eyes, you found it fit to favor me even in those times when I knew that I wasn't worthy. I am forever grateful for my salvation. I vow to serve you until the day You call me home.

APPENDIX A

SALVATION

I could never have had this testimony today had I not known the LORD Jesus Christ as my personal LORD and Savior. My walking in obedience to His will in the difficult circumstances of my illness enabled me to pick lessons from this faith journey. You will never know the fullness of the LORD until you get to accept Him into your life. You may say a prayer like this one:

"LORD Jesus, I come to you just as I am. You loved the idea of me and so created me, for that I am glad. You already accepted me and loved me even before I existed on this earth. You died for me and paid for all of my sins.

I realize that I have broken your laws and I have been separated me from you because of my sins. I am truly sorry. I want to turn away from my sinful past and start afresh. I want to experience all that you have in store for me because Your Word has told me that you have plans for me. They are good plans with a good end. I turn away from my own plans and sinful ways and decide to follow your ways.

Please forgive me and help me avoid sinning again. LORD Jesus, I believe that you died for my sins. You resurrected from the dead, you are alive, and you hear my prayer. I invite You, LORD Jesus, to become the LORD of my life, to rule and reign in my heart from this day forward. Please send Your Holy Spirit to help me obey you and do your will for the rest of my life. In Jesus' name I pray, Amen."

Then what?

If you've prayed this prayer of salvation with true conviction, know that this is a communication between your spirit and the Spirit of the LORD. Therefore, in your emotions or your body, you may not feel any different. Yet in your spirit, an eternal change has taken place. It is like a little seed that must be watered and nurtured until it grows.

You are now a follower of Jesus Christ. This is a fact, whether or not you feel any different. What you need to do from this day is begin to talk to the LORD Jesus, to the Holy Spirit on a regular basis. That is one way of prayer.

He is a Friend who sticks closer than a brother. You can share with Him anything and everything. He, too, is happy to share back and speak to you. Ask Him for a listening ear so that you can recognize when He speaks to you.

If you want to know this God whom you have invited into your life, **read the Bible**. It's through reading His Word that you can know Him well.

Nowadays, there are so many versions of the Bible. You can get one which is easy enough for you to understand. You do not have to read the King James Version with all that ancient English. It is just one of the numerous versions. There is the Message Bible, Living Bible Translation, New Literal Translation, New King James Version, New American Standard Bible, and Contemporary English Version.

Even when you go to the Internet, you can find websites for Bible programs with numerous translations (e.g., **www.bibles.com**). Read your Bible on a regular basis. That is the food that your soul and spirit needs in order to know and grow in the LORD.

Diagnosis: Cancer

Make the Holy Spirit your closest friend. Ask Him any question and He will always bring an answer. As you read, always ask the Holy Spirit to come and teach you. He is our Helper, Teacher, Guide and Comforter. Even when you do not understand, keep reading. In time, you will begin to understand the revelation and interpretation of what you are reading.

To help you study some scriptures that can encourage you, I recommend that you get a copy of the journal that goes with this publication. It is a useful tool for spiritual growth in faith. In it, you can write your reflections on a daily basis. It also contains scriptures and some prayer directions pertaining especially to divine health.

There are numerous Bible study materials on different topics. Ask the Holy Spirit to guide you which one you need at each stage of your spiritual growth process. More importantly, **find a fellowship** where you can meet with other believers of the LORD Jesus. Again, ask the Holy Spirit to lead you. He knows your needs.

There are numerous churches and ministries emphasizing on so many aspects of the Word of God. Some are focused on faith, others are focused on divine miracles and signs, some are focused on teaching, and some on missions.

The God Who created you and put in your particular equipping knows exactly what your spiritual needs are for every season. He will guide you into a fellowship where you will grow and be blessed, and become a blessing to others also.

And finally, control your atmosphere. You are a newborn baby Christian. Maybe, you have rededicated your life to the LORD. Guard that spiritual space.

Remember what you have read in the previous chapter concerning the power of words to build up or destroy, to give life or bring death. The words you speak, the words you hear, the words you allow in your atmosphere will influence your growth positively or negatively. Choose the words you speak and the ones that are spoken to you.

Today, we live in a generation where you can find a Christian alternative to everything that the world has tried to offer. There is beautiful life-giving Christian entertainment in every format. There are many Christian brothers and sisters who will build your life. There is a number of Christian reading materials in every genre.

You have a world of opportunities to discover as you seek to control your atmosphere and begin your faith journey to your destiny in God! Remember to always ask the Holy Spirit and He will guide you.

If you need some advice or guidance in any area of your spiritual journey, you may send an email to:

myfaithjourney@aliciaproductions.com
alicia@BethelBusinessSolutions.com

APPENDIX B

JESUS HEALS DIVERSELY

I mentioned in a previous chapter about my struggle with treatment through medical technology, as opposed to what is referred to as "faith healing." I also made mention of my godmother's wisdom in encouraging me to attend hospital when necessary.

Jesus Christ definitely wants us to be well. He went through the Passion of the Cross for hours and had His body broken and bruised. The Bible specifically mentions that it is by His stripes that we are healed in our bodies and souls (Isaiah 53:5). By His death on the Cross, we were saved in our spirit. Every point in His entire experience on earth has an implication to our total life experience. Right from the time He was arrested to when He resurrected, He paid it all for us.

During His ministry on earth, the LORD Jesus Christ had performed countless miraculous healings; however, you might notice a difference in each of them. Take for instance, the healing of blind eyes. There are those whom He spoke to and their eyesight was restored. There are those whom He touched and their eyes were opened at once. There are those whom He touched twice before they could see clearly. There are those whom He mixed His spittle with dirt and applied it to the blind man's eyes, and told him to go and wash in the pool, before his eyesight was restored. The end result is this: According to their faith, they were healed, and the glory belonged to the LORD. The LORD can use any method to bring healing.

Diagnosis: Cancer

It is the LORD who created the plants from which most health-giving food and medication is extracted. It is He who gave man the wisdom to develop medicine for healing diseases. By the way, Luke, the writer of one third of the New Testament, was a practicing medical doctor in their time.

In Revelations 22:2, John the Revelator speaks of the River of Life and the Tree of Life which bears twelve fruits, one for each month. Then he wrote, "...and its leaves are for the healing of the nations." We know that in heaven, we will need no healing. The leaves from that tree are for the healing of the nations today. I took advantage of the diverse healings that come from the Tree of Life.

Jesus Christ has many leaves for healing. My journey is just one example of His healing. God prescribed my medical treatment and thus, He put destiny helpers all along the way. I had a pleasant staff around me, people who encouraged me when I was down. Even when I was alone and could not bear the pain, He carried me. When I did not finish all the seven rounds of chemo, it was because that was His prescription.

Do not think that the reason why you are undergoing such treatment in the hospital is because you do not have faith. The LORD can use the medical profession just as effectively as He can heal you instantaneously.

What you need to know is this: Is it the LORD's prescription for you to go to hospital? Is it the LORD's prescription for you to receive divine healing through prayer alone or by other means?

Go back to Him and seek Him until He speaks to you. It is His desire for you to be well and to prosper your health. He is ultimately the Great Physician and will give the correct prescription.

Medical treatment was my prescribed journey and I saw Him through every step of it. Through my experience, I saw the LORD use the medical profession to bring healing and a new meaning of life to countless people.

What it did to me was create a burden to pray for those who are in the medical profession. They have the potential to turn lives around and give hope where there has been hopelessness.

My desire now is to pray for those people who do not know how to infect others with life and hope, like the nurse who invariably instilled fear in me when I called to inquire about my colonoscopy test results.

It makes me ask the LORD to continue giving wisdom and revelation to medical researchers, more so to those who seek Him, to discover more ways to save lives using moral and humane methods.

It has given me a burden to pray for those who abuse the noble profession of medical science for immoral and inhumane methods of research in the pursuit to save lives.

Diagnosis: Cancer

APPENDIX C

PRETTY LACES, PRETTY FACES LLC

Pretty Laces, Pretty Faces, LLC is inspired by founder and co-owner, Alicia Griffin. In 2010, Alicia was diagnosed with Stage 3 cancer. Immediately following the diagnosis, the treatment regimen involving chemotherapy and radiation began. Alicia endured many months or treatment, surgeries, and recuperation.
The vision to help others gave Alicia the courage and strength to turn this tragedy into triumph.

Today, Alicia is proud to proclaim that the cancer is in remission. Alicia has dedicated her life to helping cancer patients, as well as the others who are afflicted by certain illnesses, to bring out their inner beauty and feel revitalized.

The goal of *Pretty Laces, Pretty Faces, LLC* is to help the woman of any age, nationality, and background to increase her self-esteem and confidence in her natural beauty. *Pretty Laces, Pretty Faces, LLC* offers multiple services including assisting cancer patients in ordering and applying custom lace front wigs. We also organize and participate in cancer awareness events.

If you would like to donate to our patients, you may contact the following:

Pretty Laces, Pretty Faces LLC
9714 N. 56th St. Temple
Terrace, Fl 33617
Phone: 813-985-7282
Web: www.prettylacesprettyfaces.com
Email: info@prettylacesprettyfaces.com

BETHEL BUSINESS SOLUTIONS

The vision of Bethel Business Solutions is to help every client take his or her ideas and dreams and turn them into reality. This is done by offering assistance and services through each step of the business start-up process. Credit counseling services are also available to assist clients.

It Bethel Business Solutions' goal that every client that comes through our door leaves empowered and enriched entrepreneurs. Their mission is to provide our clients with the right opportunity and efficient tools to successfully start their businesses. Bethel Business Solutions prides themselves on *Transforming Dreams into Reality.*

For further information and assistance, you may contact:

Bethel Business Solutions
1502 W. Busch Blvd, Suite B
Tampa, Fl 33612
Phone: 813-374-2427
Fax: 813-354-4730
Web: www.bethelbusinesssolutions.com
Email: Alicia@bethelbusinesssolutions.com

APPENDIX D SCIENCE

VS INSTINCT

What do you do when science states one thing but your instinct or that still small voice says something else that doesn't align with science? In chapters one and two Alicia talks about all of the warning signals and medical checkups she underwent. Alicia explains how over the years she would see many physicians and would be advised of a mere case of hemorrhoids. It was that still small voice that was constantly telling her to get a colonoscopy. Based on science Alicia was, in fact, too young to have colon cancer. Symptoms began when she was thirty years old and worsened at the age of thirty nine. It was then when she was informed that there was no way a perfectly healthy young lady like herself could have colon cancer, but she DID!

If you are experiencing blood in your stool and occasional cramping in your lower abdomen, immediately go get a checkup. If the symptoms worsen, schedule a colonoscopy.

Medical insurance usually doesn't pay for a colonoscopy unless you are at least fifty years of age or unless you are referred by a physician to the specialist.

Colon cancer is a cancer that develops in the colon or rectum and normally begins as small polyps. Few people experience symptoms of colon cancer although most people do not.

Colon cancer usually is detected in men and women ages 50 and older.

Diagnosis: Cancer

The exact cause of colon cancer is unknown; however, doctors have concluded that certain factors increase your risk of developing it, Including:

> *Family history of colon cancer
> *Polyps in colon
> *A diet that is high in fat
> *Chronic ulcerative colitis

Symptoms include but are not limited to:
> *constipation
> *bleeding from rectum
> *loose stools
> *pencil shaped stools
> *weight loss
> *pelvic pain
> *abdominal discomfort
> * Unexplained fatigue
> *dark patches in stool

For more information about signs and symptoms of colon cancer go to: www.askhealthline.com or www.webmd.com

"Listen to that still small voice. I am so glad that I did."
— Alicia Griffin

ABOUT THE AUTHOR

To readers, one may know her as an author, entrepreneur, survivor, and a modern day superwoman. To friends and family she is known as Alicia Griffin, mother, daughter, friend, wife and hero. Born in Houston, Texas and raised in Fort Myers, FL, Alicia Griffin is the epitome of trial and triumph. At an early age Alicia faced some of the most trying times but through her faith in God and determined mentality, she found ways to rise above adversity. The struggles she endured all came with a price: Teen pregnancy at the age of sixteen, the untimely death of the father of her children by the age of eighteen and looking for love in all of the wrong places, thus resulting in five out of wedlock children by the age of twenty-four. When there was nowhere else to turn Alicia turned to God. Overtime she managed to turn her life around and was given the strength to provide for her family, the life she was never afforded.

Diagnosis: Cancer

Being diagnosed with cancer would discourage anyone from attaining their goals. But for Alicia, this was only motivation to grasp a hold of her opportunities and capitalize on them. Since defeating cancer, Alicia involved herself with many businesses and organizations such as the United States Black Chamber, Inc., Working Women of Tampa Bay and has recently started her own entrepreneur networking group BBE and mentoring group, Hidden Treasures .

Alicia Griffin lives in Tampa FL with her husband Terrence Griffin where she own and operates three businesses Bethel Business Solutions, Pretty Laces, Pretty Faces, and Alicia Productions Inc. Currently, she is working on her third book and with God by her side and the support of her family and friends she believes that she can accomplish any and everything. As she always says "The best is yet to come".

Diagnosis: Cancer

Author | Entrepreneur | Life Coach

To book Alicia Griffin for your event

Please Visit:

www.aliciagproductions.com
booking@aliciaproductions.com

www.ingramcontent.com/pod-product-compliance
Lightning Source LLC
Chambersburg PA
CBHW051828040426
42447CB00006B/419